Two Brothers, One Faith

Two Brothers, One Faith

John and Charles Wesley

David Luckman

CF4·K

10 9 8 7 6 5 4 3 2 1

Copyright © 2024 David Luckman
Paperback ISBN: 978-1-5271-1162-2
Ebook ISBN: 978-1-5271-1202-5

Published by Christian Focus Publications,
Geanies House, Fearn, Tain, Ross-shire,
IV20 1TW, Scotland, U.K.
www.christianfocus.com;
email: info@christianfocus.com

Cover design by Daniel van Straaten
Cover illustration by Graham Kennedy
Printed and bound by Nørhaven, Denmark

Scripture quotations are from The Holy Bible, English
Standard Version, copyright © 2001 by Crossway Bibles,
a publishing ministry of Good News Publishers. Used by
permission. All rights reserved. esv Text Edition: 2011.

Contents

Fire! Fire! 7

A Good Education 15

The Holy Club 25

Storms at Sea 33

Secretary for Indian Affairs 43

Chaplain in Savannah 57

My Chains Fell Off 67

Preaching Outdoors 79

In the Mission Field 89

Riots and Opposition 99

Across the Irish Sea 107

Love and Marriage 119

A Time of Grief 129

Give God the Glory 139

Fact File 148

John and Charles Wesley Timeline 156

Thinking Further Topics 158

Fire! Fire!

Hetty rolled over in bed, feeling all warm and toasty under the sheets. As she settled onto her right side, she heard a crackling sound above her head. It was coming from the wooden beams of the attic. Rolling on to her back she slowly opened her eyes. The beams appeared to be smouldering. Smoke was swirling around them. Perhaps she was dreaming. She rubbed her eyes to make sure. No, it was really happening. A small piece of burning ash floated down from the ceiling and landed gently on her bedspread. Hetty quickly jumped out of bed and ran to her parents in the master bedroom.

'Papa! Mama!' she screamed, as she burst through the bedroom doors. 'The house is on fire!'

Samuel and Susanna Wesley woke suddenly and looked at their daughter who was pulling the bedding off them as she raised the alarm. Samuel got out of bed first. It was more difficult for his wife, Susanna, as she was eight months pregnant. By now the fire had taken hold of their home and there was no time to dress. Samuel and Susanna rushed into the girls' room. They needed to escape immediately. Any hesitation could cost them their lives. The house was made of timber and plaster. The roof was thatched with straw. They only had moments to get out of the growing inferno.

'Take Hetty and get out now, Susanna. Be careful on the stairs!' commanded Samuel before running to the nursery calling out to the nurse to save herself and the children.

A fourteenth-month-old Charles was bundled out of his cot while Patty and the other children followed the nurse as fast as they could. Nancy and Molly met their anxious father on the landing.

'Emily! Sukey! Get up! It's a fire!' bellowed Samuel to his two eldest girls in the other bedroom.

By now the fire was advancing aggressively. The air was dense with smoke. It was getting harder to breathe. Samuel ushered his family down the stairs. Moments later they arrived in the garden, a welcome refuge from the furnace. But where were Emily and Sukey?

Without any regard for her own safety, Susanna tried to go back into the flaming building to rescue her remaining children. Three times she attempted to wade through the intensifying fire, only to suffer burns to her legs and face in the process. She was distraught. Where were the eldest girls?

When they had heard their father's warning. Emily had walked to the door of their room and opened it. With no one on the landing she assumed everyone was outside.

'It's a fire, Sukey!' she screamed.

'Can we get down the stairs?' asked Sukey. Emily looked again, only to see thick plumes of black smoke rising up the staircase.

'No. It's too dangerous now,' replied Emily.

'It'll have to be the window,' said Sukey. She opened it as wide as it would go. A growing number of neighbours were gathering around the rectory to help. Sukey stuck her legs out of the window, holding on to the window ledge until her arms were fully extended. The drop to the path wasn't too far away from her feet. She let go and landed safely on the ground.

'Come on Emily!' she shouted. 'Do what I did!' Emily copied her sister's technique and fell to the ground, thankfully without hurting herself.

The two girls ran to find the rest of the family. Susanna grabbed them and hugged them tightly. She looked at Samuel. 'Have we got them all?' she asked.

Samuel checked the group of children about him. There were seven. There should be eight.

'Where is Jacky?' asked Susanna worriedly. John, or Jacky as the family called him, was missing.

Samuel rushed selflessly into the flames to save his son. He was repelled by the intense heat. He tried again, only to be beaten back by the fierce heat. In defeat and grief, Samuel gathered his remaining family around him in the garden.

'Come, come, children. Let us kneel and pray for Jacky. Let us commend the dear boy into God's eternal rest,' he sobbed, as the tears ran down his scorched cheeks. The Wesley family knelt down to pray.

Upstairs in the nursery, John had finally woken up. He slept in a little canopy bed that was surrounded by curtains. The commotion did not stir him from his slumber immediately. It was the light of the blaze that aroused him.

'Nanna! Nanna!' he called out. There was no response from the nurse. 'Nanna, can you come to me?' he pleaded. John poked his little head through the curtains. He saw streaks of fire dancing on the ceiling of the nursery. He swiftly clambered out of his bed and ran to the nursery door. The floor outside the nursery was savagely burning and John knew he couldn't go that way. He turned back into the room and climbed on to a wooden chest that was underneath his bedroom window. John's slight figure at the window was spotted by a neighbour outside the house.

'Look! Up there at the window! I see a boy!' he exclaimed. 'I'll get a ladder.'

'There's no time for that,' shouted another neighbour. 'I have thought of something else. I'll stand against the wall. Get a light man to stand on my shoulders. We should be high enough to pull the boy from the window.'

The man fixed his hands firmly on the wall and stood with his legs apart to strengthen his stance. Another man was helped by some others onto the shoulders of the first. Seeing the plan, John opened the window. The flames had taken over the roof completely. Billowing smoke shot upwards into the cold night sky.

'Young master Wesley, lean forward out of the window and extend your arms,' coaxed the light man as he straightened up. 'Do not fear. I will hold you.'

John did as his rescuer ordered. The man grabbed hold of John's arms and hoisted him almost brutally out of the window and grasped him tightly. At that precise moment, the roof collapsed inward to the nursery. The onlookers gasped with shock as the clatter of the disintegrating roof filled their ears. The men scrambled as fast as they could away from the crumbling house.

'Jacky!' cried Susanna. She grabbed the lad from the brave men who had saved him and held him tightly in her arms. All of a sudden, it turned into a group hug, as each member of the Wesley household clung to each other in the garden. They were shivering despite the heat from the emblazoned wreck which was their home only a few minutes before.

Samuel was overwhelmed with relief and gratitude. He could hardly believe it. He smothered Jacky with kisses just to be sure he was truly alive. He then turned to the crowd.

'Come, my neighbours. Let us kneel down and give thanks to God,' he implored. 'God has given me all my eight children. Let the house go. I am rich enough,'[1]

---

1. Samuel's words, from *John Wesley, Into All The World*, by John Telford, page 18.

he continued, smiling at his children as they embraced one another.

Some neighbours joined the Wesleys in a short prayer of thanksgiving to God for the safe rescue of the family. Then they retreated further from the blaze and watched in horrified stillness as the house disintegrated before their eyes. Although Samuel was concerned that the distress caused by the fire might do harm to Susanna and their unborn baby, he was confident that God would give him his nineteenth child.

'Samuel,' said Susanna, 'the children are exhausted. I am tired too. We need somewhere to sleep.'

'I shall see if any of the neighbours can accommodate us tonight,' Samuel replied. He left her side for only a short moment. Offers to help the Wesleys were not hard to find that night. The children were farmed out to their neighbours who were willing to give them a bed for the night.

The next morning Samuel Wesley went to inspect the charred remains of his home. The ashes were smouldering in the cold February air. It was immediately clear to him that everything was lost in the fire that night. However, Samuel's heart was still rejoicing that his family, his greatest treasure, was safe and sound, thanks be to God! But he couldn't help wondering how it was started in the first place.

When Samuel first arrived in the market-town of Epworth in the spring of 1697 as the new minister for St Andrew's Church, the Wesley family received a warm welcome from the community. Samuel junior was seven years old at the time and settled in well to life in Epworth. Emily, Sukey and Molly liked being there too. But not long after their arrival, in 1702, there was a fire at the rectory destroying a large part of the house. Fortunately it was easy to repair. At the time, Samuel suspected a disgruntled parishioner had started the blaze in his linseed field next to the house but couldn't prove anything.

As Samuel picked through the rectory remains, he couldn't help wondering if perhaps another neighbour wanted him to leave the parish. But he was determined to rebuild the house though there would be no financial assistance from the Church of England to do it. If he was going to pay for a new house he would rebuild the rectory out of bricks. Nothing says, 'I'm staying in Epworth' like a sturdy brick house, he thought.

Among the charred timbers on the ground he noticed the corner of a page from one of his Bibles. He picked it up and shook off the ash that obscured some of the writing. He could just about make out the verse from one of the Gospels. It read, 'Go, sell all that you have and take up your cross and follow me.' A very appropriate word from the Lord, he thought. He would endure come what may for the sake of his Master.

As for the children? There was nothing else for it, he thought, 'They will have to live with relatives and friends for the duration of the build.'

***

The Wesley family were separated until the new brick rectory was completed towards the end of 1709. When the family reassembled, Susanna was horrified at how the children had lapsed in their studies and behaviour. Each home in which the children resided had different routines and disciplines, or lack thereof in some cases. She must sort that out at once.

You see, before the fire at the Epworth rectory, the children enjoyed a daily regime of arduous learning. There was little time for frivolous activities like jumping in muddy puddles when it rained or catching frogspawn in the local waters surrounding Epworth. Mrs Wesley's children were expected to study for six hours each day. Susanna taught them how to read as soon as they were able to recite the alphabet, which was usually a day or two after their fifth birthdays. The children learned the Lord's Prayer at an early age. They read the Bible together and prayed together every day.

Susanna expected good manners from all her beloved children. They were not allowed to shout. There were no snacks between meals in the day. The Wesley clan was not permitted to play with other boys and girls from the town. And they couldn't take things without getting permission from the person who owned it.

Now that they were back together, Susanna would soon lick them all into shape again.

A Good Education

The Wesley children thrived under the instruction of their devoted mother. About five years after the rectory fire, when John was only ten years old, his parents decided it was time for him to leave the small town of Epworth for the bustling city of London. John Sheffield, the Duke of Buckingham, was a friend of the family. He sponsored John for entrance into Charterhouse School. Samuel and Susanna were thrilled at the prospect of their Jacky going to such a wonderful establishment in the nation's capital. Charterhouse School was over a hundred years old, with a decent reputation among the educated people of London society.

Jacky was armed with much parental advice for his life at school. There was one piece in particular that he took to heart. His father encouraged him to run around the school grounds three times every morning before breakfast. A healthy body helps to provide concentration for study and gives stamina for a long school day. Jacky could see the benefit of this and without fail, he did as his father instructed. And sure enough, his father was right.

John, as he was known outside the family, applied himself in class to learning the Greek and Latin classics. He excelled in these subjects. It seemed that he had a knack for learning. He attributed his schooling successes to his mother's loving and robust attention to her children's education at home.

Charterhouse was blighted with the ancient problem of bullying on a grand scale. The older boys were engaged in a daily routine of forcefully taking the lunch meat from the younger and smaller boys. John survived on bread for lunch during his time at Charterhouse. Despite this, he remained in good health, although he was not big in physical stature.

Every morning and evening Jacky read the Bible and prayed. However, he paid little heed to what he learned as he went about his business the rest of the day. When he was at home in Epworth, he was taught that if he wanted to be saved by God from an eternity in hell, then he needed to keep all of God's commandments. He tried hard to keep them and be a good boy. He wanted to please his parents and please God too. Yet at Charterhouse, he could see for himself that he wasn't trying as hard as he did at home. In fact, he was blatantly disobeying many of the commandments of God – nothing outrageous of course – he wasn't as bad as some of his friends.

Still, his own view of God's salvation changed slightly. Now he believed he would be saved by God if he wasn't as bad as other people and if he kept up the appearance of liking religion. He would also keep reading the Bible, and he would go to church and pray. These are good things to do. Surely if he did all this then God would be happy with him. Good works will get him into heaven, he believed. He was unaware that salvation is by grace alone through faith alone in Christ alone.[1]

In 1716, when John was at Charterhouse for two years, his younger brother Charles was preparing to head off to Westminster School in London. This excellent school was adjacent to the famous Westminster Abbey in the centre of the city. Leaving the security of home in Epworth, his mother and father, and his siblings, was very daunting for the eight-year-old Charles. Of course, he was excited too. His older brother Samuel had gone to Westminster School when he was a boy. Then he went to study at Oxford University. Samuel returned to Westminster School for a job as the assistant to the Schoolmaster around the same time that John started at Charterhouse School. Samuel told Charles that he could stay with him and his wife at Westminster. Charles couldn't wait to spend time with his older brother and Aunt Ursula, or 'Nutty' as everyone called her.

'Aunt Nutty – that's funny,' giggled Charles. 'I wonder if she is a bit nutty too. I do hope so! It will be so much fun if she is!' he exclaimed to Kezzy while they were playing together in the nursery. Kezzy was

---

1. Ephesians 2:1-10.

the baby in Susanna's tummy at the time of the rectory fire. She came into the world shortly after the dreadful event.

'Nutty!' bellowed Kezzy. They both started to belly laugh. Little amuses the innocent.

***

Charles settled in well to life at Westminster School. He studied the Greek and Latin classics and was a good student, just like his brother John. Much to his dismay, he had to be careful around his Aunt Nutty, as she proved to be more severe with him than playful. Nonetheless he loved being with Samuel, who acted more like his father than his brother at times. Charles didn't mind that. He admired and respected both his older brothers, especially John, who was beginning to show the qualities of a good leader.

It came as no surprise when John got a scholarship to go to Oxford University in 1720. Just a week after he turned seventeen, on 24 June, he made the journey to Christ Church College in the town of Oxford. His parents were delighted that they had another son who was going to Oxford. John was a serious lad who studied hard. He had a good reputation amongst his peers for knowing the classical works and he was a good writer. He liked art, too.

On a cold winter's day during his time in Oxford, a knock came to his study door. John was hanging some paintings that he had just purchased from a local dealership. He opened the door to reveal a young chambermaid.

'Hello, hello,' said John heartily. 'It is good to see you. Won't you come in, my dear?' he asked politely.

'Yes. Thank you, sir,' she replied. John noticed that she was shivering. She wore a light linen gown. It was not thick enough to keep out the cold.

'You look half-starved,' he said, noticing her gaunt appearance. 'Have you nothing to cover you but that thin linen gown?' he asked, pointing to her inadequate winter clothing.

'This is all I have, sir,' she replied.

John was distressed at her news. He reached into his pocket to give her some money for food and a coat. He pulled out his hand and saw he had barely any left after his recent purchases. Straight away he knew in his heart that God was not pleased with how he was spending his money. The girl could see by the look on his face how disappointed he was in himself.

'Thank you anyway, sir,' she said appreciatively. But John knew his good intentions did nothing to help her situation.

In the quietness of his own mind, he chastised himself. 'Will your Master say to you, "*Well done, good and faithful steward?*"' to which John knew the resounding answer was, 'of course not!' His reprimand of himself continued, 'You have decorated your walls using the money which would have protected this poor girl from the cold!' John looked at his new paintings as the rebuke went on. 'O justice! O mercy! Are not these pictures the blood of this poor maid?'[2] He was distraught that his paintings prevented him from helping the girl in her hour of need. From that moment on, John Wesley was resolute in helping the poor of society as much as he could. He would give away as much money as he could from his own pocket.

***

Susanna and Samuel Wesley were very proud of their three sons. All of them were diligent and successful in their studies. After graduating with a Bachelor of Arts degree from Christ Church, they encouraged John to consider ordination for ministry in the Church of England. He became a clergyman in autumn of 1725. The following spring, John was given the distinguished title of Fellow of Lincoln College, located in the heart of Oxford. He became a lecturer there. In October, that year, his brother Charles arrived as a new student in Christ Church, Oxford, having been awarded a King's Scholarship which paid for his education. Charles was eighteen years old.

Charles experienced a new found freedom at Christ Church. He was no longer under the watchful eye of his oldest brother. He wanted to indulge his desires in the same way that John had at the college. He loved the idea of learning new things, but he couldn't bear the hard slog required to learn them. His love of poetry shone through, especially when he burst into John's rooms at Lincoln College to recite a sonnet. He also loved to see what John was working on, and often rummaged

---

2. From John Wesley's *Sermon On Dress*, Boston 1800, page 13.

through the papers strewn around his desk. He annoyed John when he did this. John was also worried about his brother's lack of religious seriousness.

'There is something I want to ask you, Charles.'

'Oh, this sounds serious, brother.'

'It has come to my attention that you lack diligence with your Bible reading and prayer.'

'Who told you that?' Charles was less bothered about religion than his brother.

'I have seen how frivolous you seem these days, especially in matters of religion.'

'Do not think for one moment that just because you are now a clergyman, you are closer to God than I, dear brother.'

'But I think I am, brother. Are you not concerned about your salvation?'

'What, would you have me a saint all at once?' The conversation was getting tense. 'I shall hear no more of this,' added Charles, and stormed out of the room.

The conversation shook Charles. He did not like fighting with John. It upset him. Over the next few days, John's words bore into his soul. Perhaps his older brother was right. Perhaps he did need to be more serious about the things of God. He knew for sure that he did not want to disagree with John like that again. He decided he would tell John how he felt. He penned a short letter expressing how forlorn he was feeling from the conversation and that he was determined never to argue with his brother again.

Back at Epworth, Samuel Wesley Sr was struggling with the work load. He needed an assistant and looked to his son John for help. Lincoln College treated John well and gave him some time off to enable him to go back to Epworth and work as his father's curate. The college arranged with John that he could renew his leave of absence every six months. John was welcome to return to Oxford anytime he wanted.

John left to go back home in the August of 1727. Meanwhile, in Christ Church College, his brother Charles was starting to take his studies and his faith, more seriously. However, the college was a difficult place for anyone looking to follow God's commands.

One evening, on the 5th of May 1729, he sat at his desk and by candlelight, wrote to John back in Epworth:

> John,
> I confess that for thirteen years I have never really been attentive to public prayer at church. I cannot therefore expect to find any warmth of religion at college. But I will look upon the coldness I experience here as a trial. I will not go back to the way I was, although I am afraid that if I have no good business of my own, the Devil will soon find me some mischief to attend to. I am sure it is because of mother's influence that I think the way I do now. I cannot recall how or when I woke out of my lethargy for living to please God, although I suspect that it was not long after you went away from Oxford and back home. I am of the strong opinion that I must find a group of like-minded men here, to encourage and support the work of God in our lives. I earnestly pray for this, and I covet your prayers, too, brother.[3]
> Charles

---

3. Paraphrased by the author, from *Charles Wesley as Revealed in his Letters*, by Frank Baker, page 13.

Charles identified two men in the Oxford colleges who possessed a similar desire to serve and please God in their lives. He approached Robert Kirkham who was studying at Merton College in Oxford. He also spoke to William Morgan, from Dublin in Ireland, who was studying at Christ Church College with him. Charles persuaded these two men of the spiritual benefit of meeting every week to read the Bible and pray together. He was thrilled when they agreed to do it.

Lincoln College needed John to return, in order to supervise and tutor some new students. In November 1729, he bade his parents farewell and entered once again into the academic life of Oxford.

Charles was euphoric at John's return to Oxford. He excitedly introduced John to his friends and at once the four men began to meet a few evenings a week to study the New Testament together in the original Greek language that it was written in. Charles willingly relinquished the leadership of the group to John.

The 'Holy Club' was established.

The Holy Club

The Castle Prison and the Bocardo were the accommodation for the town of Oxford's lawbreakers. Most of them were poor and smelled awful due to a lack of personal hygiene. Sickness and disease were never far away from those who lived in the Oxford prisons. The causes for incarceration ranged from as little as an inability to pay a debt, to the violent and despicable act of murder.

Generally the prisons in England were in an awful state. The wardens were corrupt and useless. Often prisoners faced excessive and brutal discipline at the hands of guards. It was into this dark closed world that William Morgan confidently strode with a Bible in his hand and compassion in his heart for the lost souls of the Oxford prison system. He started to visit a man who had murdered his wife. William was intent on telling him about the love of God that is available to all who were willing to repent of their wicked ways and follow the Master. Yes, even murder was forgivable by God if there was true repentance in the heart of the penitent person. William visited the man on a number of occasions. He was convinced of the need for such an important ministry. He would speak to John about it.

'You have been doing this a while, William,' said John.

'Yes. I have been visiting a poor wretch at the castle who took the life of his wife a while back. He is very sorrowful and is expecting the magistrate to deliver a sentence that fits his crime. He feels he deserves nothing less.'

'Does he appreciate your visits?'

'Yes. He seems to. We have had some good conversations about God.' William paused briefly and then went on, 'John, I think there is a lot of good to do in the prisons if anyone would be willing now and again to speak with the prisoners.'

John knew what William was inferring. 'I am not sure it would be a fitting thing for an Oxford don to accompany Oxford students on prison visitations.' William appeared irked. He did not want to carry this ministerial burden on his own. After all, the Holy Club was there to support one another to holy living and good deeds. John could see the disappointment on his friend's face. He told William that he was prepared to seek some advice from his father and the Bishop of Oxford on the matter.

The responses were overwhelmingly positive from both men. Mr Wesley was delighted that his boys should consider such a worthwhile cause. The Bishop of Oxford was pleased to hear that such a worthwhile ministry was to be undertaken in his diocese. It was settled then. Charles and John would go with William Morgan to the prisons.

The little society of men grew in reputation and numbers over the next couple of years, until there were nine men from the colleges of Oxford attending the Holy Club, including a young man called George Whitefield and another Benjamin Ingham.

The men of the Holy Club engaged themselves in many good works. They visited prisoners in the castle and the poor people of the city. They helped neglected children go to school and learn to read and write. They cared for the sick and needy. They gave out prayer books and Bibles when they had the money. Being faithful Church of England men, whatever they did in the service of God, they did with the permission of the Bishop of Oxford.

Under John's leadership and example, the men sought to order their lives. They got up early each day to pray. They fasted on Wednesdays and Fridays. They received the Lord's Supper together every week at college. They had a set prayer to say at nine, twelve and three each day, along with stated times for private meditation and prayer. They engaged regularly in a form of spiritual self-examination. They asked themselves whether they had been zealous to do good works; or to keep the commands of the Church and the University; or if they had shown kindness to everyone or prayed for all around them.

Their actions around college and in Oxford did not go unnoticed. They were hated and ridiculed. Along with the label of the 'Holy Club', they were given the nickname 'Methodists' because of their desire to be 'methodical' in their lifestyle and worship.

In all of it, the fledgling group of Methodists thought that fasting and praying, doing good to others, visiting prisoners, caring for the sick and needy, helping the poor somehow would save their souls. They were trying to please God and save themselves by doing good things, rather than trusting in the finished work of Christ on the cross for salvation. John and Charles Wesley knew little of the pure gospel of Jesus Christ.

***

The message came that Samuel Wesley Sr was terribly unwell. John and Charles made haste to Epworth to be close to him and their mother. During his last hours, the two brothers sat at his bedside, with the others close by. Charles leaned forward in prayer, then he felt the hand of his father come to rest on his head.

'Be steady,' exhorted Samuel softly. Charles looked up to meet the serene gaze of his ailing father. 'The Christian faith will surely revive in this kingdom,' Samuel continued. 'You shall see it, but I shall not.'

'Yes, father,' agreed Charles, attempting a small smile at his ailing father.

Samuel Wesley Sr died on 25th April, 1735. He was seventy-two years old. Three days later the Wesley family had a simple funeral in St Andrews. They laid the body of their father in the graveyard. It was what he wanted.

Little did Samuel know how true his words to Charles were and that God would use his two sons to help bring about a spiritual awakening in Britain and Ireland. However, they had another trial to pass through in America before God would use the young Methodists in a great revival of their own land.

The colony of Georgia was set up in 1732 by Colonel James Oglethorpe. A former soldier and Member of Parliament, the colonel was concerned about the suffering experienced by poor people who got themselves into debt, couldn't afford to pay, and were subsequently thrown into prison. He was able to use his influence as a politician to get many of them released. His sympathy for the poor inspired a practical solution for their benefit, and the colony was established in America.

Newly released prisoners were invited to start afresh in the colonel's colony in America. Invitations were extended to anyone who could provide a meaningful service to the newly formed Georgian society. Oglethorpe named it Georgia, in honour of the King of England, George II.

John Wesley received a personal request from the colonel to join him in his American endeavour. The Society for the Propagation of the Gospel, or S.P.G., offered John the chaplaincy in the capital of Georgia, called Savannah. It was the official overseas missionary society of the Church of England. The S.P.G. also offered him £50.00 a year for his work there. It was roughly the same amount of money that a clergyman would get for looking after a small parish in England.

John sought the advice of some family and friends. Susanna Wesley was thrilled at the news and encouraged him to go. However, he did not want to go alone. He would ask his brother Charles to join him. On the one hand, Charles had no desire to leave Oxford, but he loved being with his brother so, it was easy for John to persuade him to go to America. Not only that, he also encouraged Charles to seek ordination as a Church of England clergyman before they left.

Two other young Methodists joined them on their adventure, Benjamin Ingham and Charles Delamotte. So this merry band were ready to travel to America on a mission from God. The reality, however, was that they all hoped they would save their own souls by preaching the gospel to the unconverted in that faraway place.

In preparation for America, Charles was ordained as a clergyman a couple of weeks before the departure from England. He had been assigned the role of Secretary for Indian Affairs and minister to the colonists. He was also to be the personal secretary to Colonel Oglethorpe in Georgia.

On Tuesday 14th October 1735, the men travelled to the town of Gravesend in Kent, to board the ship that would carry them across the Atlantic to the East Coast of America.

The *Simmonds* weighed over two hundred tonnes and was capable of carrying 257 people as well as cargo. Another large ship called the *London Merchant* was scheduled to make the journey at the same time. They would be escorted on their journey by a naval *man-of-war* known as the *Hawk*.

Colonel Oglethorpe did not want the young men to be disturbed on the crossing, so gave them two cabins at the forward part of the ship. John and Charles were in one, with Ingham and Delamotte in the other slightly smaller cabin.

'We shall be quite comfortable, brother,' said Charles as he lay his cases on the floor.

'It is most adequate indeed,' added John, taking in his new surroundings.

Delamotte and Ingham walked in. 'This is a bigger room than ours,' Ingham blurted out.

'It will serve well as somewhere that the four of us can meet for prayer and study,' said Delamotte.

'We wouldn't all fit comfortably into our cabin, I'm afraid,' added Ingham.

'Yes. We shall meet here throughout our time on board,' said John. 'Remember what I said – that it will be impossible to promote the work of God among the heathen unless we are united in what we say and do.'

'So if we disagree, then we go with the majority decision,' said Charles.

'And if it is a 2-2 split we'll draw lots, and that will settle the matter.'

The others nodded to confirm their arrangement.

'We have agreed not to eat meat and drink wine during the voyage,' reminded John. 'We'll eat only rice and biscuits.'

'Speaking of food, I could eat something now,' said Delamotte. Ingham admitted to being a little peckish himself.

'I think lunch is about one. It shouldn't be too long now before we dine,' said Charles.

The men dispersed to unpack and settle themselves on board the *Simmonds*. During the week in the dock at Gravesend, they used their time productively meeting and befriending other passengers. Twenty-six passengers were German. John decided to learn their language so that he could talk with them during the voyage.

On Tuesday 21 October, 1735, the two vessels set sail from Gravesend to Cowes on the Isle of Wight. Bad weather forced a long delay there, which allowed Charles to get re-acquainted with a friend who was the clergyman at the local church. Grounded in Cowes, Charles accepted a kind invitation to preach on a few occasions. Loads of people came to church to hear him and Charles was pleased that he was able to do some good among the congregation there. However, the time came in December for the *Simmonds* to leave the fair shores of the Isle of White.

The challenging and dangerous crossing of the Atlantic to America had begun at last.

Storms at Sea

John kept a journal. It was another discipline he developed because he wanted to account for how he spent his days. He had no desire to squander time frivolously on matters that were, quite frankly, unimportant in his view. Time is on a linear path. There is a beginning to life and an end. John had set his mind to use the time in-between for the glory of God.

Sitting by the desk in his cabin on board the *Simmonds*, his journal was lit up by the oil lamp perched on the corner of the desk. He took a moment to gather his thoughts, then began to write an account of how he and his friends spent their time each day among the other emigrants to America.

'From four in the morning until five, each of us pray on our own. From five until seven, we read the Bible together in this cabin. We compare what we read with the writings of some of the early Christians, (just so we don't rely completely on our own understanding).

At seven we have breakfast.

Then at eight we gather together with some of the other passengers for public prayers.

From nine until twelve noon, I usually learn German. Mr Delamotte learns some New Testament Greek. My brother writes sermons and Mr Ingham teaches the Bible to the children on board the ship.

At twelve we meet together to talk about what we had done since our last meeting, and we talk about what we were going to do before our next meeting.

We dine at about one in the afternoon.

The time from dinner until four, we spend reading to those of whom each of us has taken charge. Or we spend that time speaking to them individually if there is a need to do that.

There are evening prayers at four. Either the second Bible reading is explained, or the children are taught Christian truths before the congregation.

From five to six we return to our cabins for private prayer.

From six to seven I read in our cabin to two or three of the passengers[1], and my friends do something similar.

At seven I join the Germans in their public service on the deck, while Mr Ingham reads the Scriptures below decks to anyone who wants to hear him.

We meet again at eight to encourage and instruct one another in our faith. Then between nine and ten each of us retire to bed. The roaring of the sea or the motion of the ship cannot wake us from the refreshing sleep that God gives us.'[2]

It was a exceptionally methodical routine, in keeping with their 'Methodist' reputation but sometimes they could not follow their schedule because of the rough seas that ravaged the ship on their journey.

In January 1736, John began a record of a quick succession of storms that truly challenged his faith in

---

1. There were about eighty English on board.
2. Paraphrased by the author, from John Wesley's *Journal - Volume 1*, page 17, entry for Tuesday 21st October, 1735.

God. On Saturday, 17 January, John and Charles had been invited into the cabin of Colonel Oglethorpe. A wind was blowing against the direction of the ship all day. Many ship's sailors and passengers were complaining of the slowness of their progress. But by seven in the evening, the wind had swelled into a full-blown storm. With each hour came bigger waves that smashed onto the side of the ship, tossing it about the ocean like a twig in a turbulent river.

'I feel most unwell,' said Charles to his company. 'I have not got the stomach for sea travel during fair weather, let alone a storm as raucous as this!'

'There is little I can do about the weather to make your journey more comfortable than I have already,' replied Oglethorpe. 'Storms in the Atlantic are a common occurrence. It would be prudent to brace ourselves.'

'I am quite sure the passengers' impatience at the slow progress today is no longer on their minds!' exclaimed John.

'There is nothing like a storm at sea to put one's focus in perspective,' Oglethorpe decreed.

Suddenly, the windows of the cabin burst open, and a deluge of seawater poured into the room. John was close to a wooden writing bureau which offered him protection. The other men were buffeted about like soggy rag dolls.

As a young boy, John hated the sea. The experience in Oglethorpe's cabin did absolutely nothing to allay his fears. He could hear the screams of passengers outside the window on the watery deck. Their cries of dread were echoed in his own heart. John did not want to die. He was not ready to die.

The tempest continued over the next few hours. Exhausted from his attempts to ride out the storm, John retreated to a bed to lie down. He felt ashamed of himself. He was a clergyman in the Church of England who preached about God and yet he was unwilling to die and be with God. Deep down, John was not sure if God would be pleased with his efforts to serve him.

'O how pure in heart must the man be, who would rejoice to appear before God at a moment's notice,' John said to himself. 'I am not such a man, to my shame.' Eventually he drifted off to sleep, wondering if he would wake up, really hoping that he would.

The following morning the storm had abated. John and the other Methodists appeared on deck to encourage their fellow travellers to give thanks to God for mercifully seeing them through a tempestuous night. Some of the sailors just shrugged their shoulders and laughed, saying that the storm was just a mild dose of inclement weather – nothing to be worried about – all in a day's work in the life of a mariner. However, to those who had never experienced a storm at sea before, like the Wesleys and their friends, it was clear that no one on board had the power to stop the wind and the waves from doing their damage. Only one man has authority over God's world in this way. Jesus Christ displayed the power and authority of God as he commanded the wind and the waves of a furious squall to be calm. Jesus spoke the words, and the wind stopped, and the waves were perfectly still.[3] Did John and Charles know this Jesus personally? The fearful event of the night before made John wonder if he truly did know Jesus Christ as Saviour and Lord.

The week after the storm, the Wesley brothers, along with Ingham and Delamotte, went about their duties on board the ship. One evening after dinner, their thoughts turned to the mission field in America. The four men gathered in the Wesleys' room.

'How do you think they will receive us in Georgia?' asked Charles.

'I think the native Indians will be like little children, humble, willing to learn and eager to do the will of God,' replied John naively. The fact was none of them really had any idea how they or the gospel of Christ would be received by the locals in Georgia. It was wishful thinking to believe they would get a warm welcome, especially when they proclaimed the uniqueness of Jesus as the only way to God the Father.[4] This truth would put the brothers at odds with the native Indians who had a different view about spiritual things. The natives believed that plants, animals, rivers, mountains, and other features of the natural world had spiritual qualities and powers.

'We have to survive the crossing first,' said Ingham drolly.

---

3. Mark 4:35-41; Psalm 107:23-31.
4. John 14:6.

Delamotte chuckled. 'I hope there are no more storms like the last one.'

'I am very happy to be a … what is the word the sailors use … a "landlubber"' said Charles and Ingham at the same time.

Unfortunately, during the evening of Friday, 23 January, another storm struck. The helmsmen did all they could to steer the ship in the right direction. However, by morning the storm had increased so much, they gave up and allowed the ship to travel in whatever direction the storm dictated.

Once again, John was afraid of an early demise. He chastised himself for his lack of faith in God.

At one o'clock that Saturday afternoon, John ventured out on deck to assess the situation for himself. The power of the waves swept him right off his feet. He lay on the deck for a moment, listening to the terrifying creaks and groans of the wooden ship.

The sheer violence of the sea's attack left John stunned. He clambered onto his feet and with small, determined steps made it back to the cabin.

John found Charles and his Oxford friends hunkered down in the Wesley's cabin, praying with all their might that the Lord would deliver them from the tempest once again.

'Don't go outside,' John said loudly from the doorway of the cabin. 'It's extremely wet out there.' He stumbled to his bed and threw himself down. It was the perfect place to wait out the storm, he decided.

Ingham smiled, knowing that John was perfectly serious about his instruction to stay inside.

At midnight, the storm was over. Everyone on board was exhausted just trying to survive the crossing. Like the rest of the passengers, the Oxford missionaries slept soundly that night.

The third storm, however, began at noon on Sunday. It picked up force by the mid-afternoon. The waves pummelled the ship's bows with intense ferocity. The passengers struggled to stand upright. They held on to anything solid that would help them.

As it was Sunday, the twenty-six Moravians[5] on board held their religious service at seven o'clock that evening. The meeting was led by their bishop, David Nitschmann. John had been impressed by the Moravians' unflappable religious zeal throughout the journey. He had set himself the task of learning some German so he could speak with his new friends, and even attend their services on board the ship.

Occasionally the Oxford missionaries witnessed the Moravians being insulted for their faith in God by other passengers or sailors. Sometimes they were physically assaulted. This behaviour neither hindered nor stopped their proclamation of the gospel on board the ship. John and Charles were most impressed with them.

The service began with psalm singing. All of a sudden their melodic song was brutally interrupted by the turbulent sea which breached the sides of the ship.

---

5. See *Fact File* on 'The Moravians' for more information.

The main sail was broken into pieces by the sharp force of the waves. The sea cascaded down through the decks of the ship and for a brief moment its inhabitants felt that the vessel had been fully submerged. But it hadn't.

The English passengers were frightened. They screamed in terror as this storm threatened to pull them down into a watery grave. However, the Moravians sang sweetly on. John could not believe how calm his German friends were, while at the same time noticing how the other passengers lamented their own destruction.

Over the next few hours the ship was tossed to and fro. As the winds slowly died down, John decided to talk with one of the Moravians about their reactions to the storm.

'Were you not afraid?' John asked.

'I thank God, no. I was not,' replied the Moravian man.

'But were your women and children not afraid?'

'No. Our women and children are not afraid to die.'

John was amazed and inspired by the answer he received. He left his friend and went to speak with some of the other passengers who were huddled together, crying, and shaking with fear, even though the storm was subsiding.

John, pointed at the Moravians. 'In this hour of trial, look at the difference between those who know and fear God and those who do not!'

It was a poignant moment for John Wesley. Which group did he belong to? Or his brother Charles for that matter? What about Ingham and Delamotte? For sure, the stormy experience on board the *Simmonds* challenged the men's faith and exposed it as weak. Did they really trust in God as an ever present help in times of trouble?[6]

The *Simmonds* anchored off the coast of Georgia on 6 February, 1736. Colonel Oglethorpe took a small boat and went to Savannah to collect Mr August Spangenberg. He was one of the pastors of the Moravian settlement there. Spangenberg was introduced to some of the passengers, including the Methodists. John took the opportunity to engage his new acquaintance in conversation. As Spangenberg had been in Savannah a while, John thought it prudent to ask him for some advice about conduct and ministry there. John was going to replace the outgoing minister of the town and any wise words would be greatly welcomed.

Spangenberg was a perceptive pastor who knew how to test the heart of any man. 'My brother, I first must ask you one or two questions,' he said. John liked being asked questions, so he was willing to hear what they were. 'Have you the witness within yourself?' A mild quizzical look came over John's face. Spangenberg elaborated what he meant with his next question. 'Does the Spirit of God bear witness with your spirit, that you are a child of God?'

John was surprised by the questions. He didn't know how to answer Spangenberg. It was obvious to the Moravian pastor that John was struggling with his questions. Perhaps a simpler question was needed.

6. Psalm 46 :1-2.

'Do you know Jesus Christ?' asked Spangenberg.

John thought for a moment, then replied, 'I know he is the Saviour of the world.'

'True. But do you know that he has saved you?'

'I hope he has died to save me.'

'Do you know yourself?'

'I do.'

John's feeble answer did not convince Spangenberg. Truthfully, John was not convinced of it either. But that was why he had agreed to travel to America.

Before he left England, John wrote a letter to an acquaintance, expressing his main reason for going.

> My chief motive for going to Georgia, to which all the rest is subordinate, is the hope of saving my own soul.[7]

Going to America would bring John and the other Oxford men closer to knowing God's salvation in Jesus Christ. The long and hard lesson they had to learn was that their good works would not bring them peace with God.

---

7. From a letter to Dr John Burton, dated 10th October 1735.

Secretary for Indian Affairs

The American State of Georgia was the focus of a centuries-old conflict between England and Spain. Three years after founding the State's capital, Savannah, Colonel James Oglethorpe established Fort Frederica to protect his southern border from potential Spanish invasions coming up from Florida, which was under Spanish control at the time. Fort Frederica was a military outpost and town which Oglethorpe named after Prince Frederick Louis, the British Prince of Wales.

Frederica was located on St Simon's Island, 100 miles south of Savannah. It was strategically built by the edge of a river, allowing the British to have the control of ship travel on it.

In 1736 forty-four men and seventy-two women and children arrived to build Fort Frederica. They fortified the entire area with a high fence surround. Inside its wooden walls, the outpost consisted of no more than a few tents and huts. This settlement was to be the home of Charles Wesley and Benjamin Ingham for the foreseeable future.

Charles was the Secretary for Indian Affairs and minister to the local settlers. However, he spent most of his time serving as the personal assistant to Oglethorpe – a position that would have been better suited to his brother John, the one Wesley who had an incredible aptitude for organisation and administration.

As soon as he arrived in Frederica, Charles got straight to work, meeting his parishioners, and calling them to evening prayer. There was no church building, so all church meetings were conducted in the open air. A number of people gathered for that first service, including Colonel Oglethorpe. Charles was encouraged by the turnout, but more so by the Bible passage he read to them: 'Continue steadfastly in prayer, being watchful in it with thanksgiving. At the same time pray also for us, that God may open a door for the word, to declare the mystery of Christ ... that I may make it clear, which is how I ought to speak. Walk in wisdom towards outsiders making the best use of the time. Let your speech always be gracious, seasoned with salt, so that you may know how you ought to answer each person ... Say to Archippus, "See that you fulfil the ministry that you have received in the Lord."'[1]

For Charles, this passage reinvigorated him and give him direction for his ministry in Frederica. He was determined to instruct his parishioners to live holy lives. Not surprisingly his attempts to make them

---

1. Colossians 4:2-6, 17.

better 'Christians' would prove unpopular. Just like his brother John, he hadn't understood that a religion focused on good works rather than the need to be born again in Christ would never be acceptable in the Lord's sight.

Nonetheless, four times a day Charles beat a large drum loudly, to call his parishioners to prayer. No one liked it. His parishioners didn't like his sermons either. They felt he was always talking about sin and God's punishment. But Charles pressed on in his duty to care for the flock which God had given him. He knew his mission was challenging. It was a new country, and a new settlement, with new people. Charles though trusted that God would give him the strength he needed to fulfil his task.

Soon after his arrival, he met two women called Mrs Hawkins and Mrs Welsh. They had travelled to Frederica with their husbands and had been passengers on board the *Simmonds*. During the crossing, the women had expressed an interest in spiritual things. Charles, however, was not convinced of the sincerity of their attentions. His suspicions did not go unnoticed by the women. They now regarded him with hostility.

Mrs Hawkins and Mrs Welsh were instrumental in dismantling Charles' upright reputation among the settlers. His demise came swiftly. On his third day in Frederica, differences sprang up between the two women. Charles tried unsuccessfully to arbitrate between them.

The following day, Charles met the maid of Mrs Hawkins. She was deeply distressed and crying because she had been struck by Mrs Hawkins.

'My dear, whatever is the matter?' asked Charles kindly.

'Nothing, sir,' replied the maid, wiping the tears from her cheeks.

'Come now. One does not cry for no reason. Tell me what it is? Perhaps I can help.'

Through watery eyes the maid looked at the compassionate expression on Charles' face.

'My mistress ... hit me!' she sobbed. 'And I need to get away,' she added.

Charles thought for a moment and then suggested, 'Perhaps I can convince you to stay. Nothing good ever came from running away from the difficulties in life. They need to be met head on. Let me take you back to Mrs Hawkins, and I will mediate for you.'

'No, sir, no. I cannot go back. Mrs Hawkins has a bad temper and I do not want to be on the receiving end of it anymore.'

'You exaggerate, my dear. Mrs Hawkins may be indelicate at times, but ...'

'But you haven't seen her when she gets in a rage,' interrupted the maid.

It took Charles a while to calm the maid and convince her to remain in Frederica. She reluctantly agreed to stay and went with him to the lodgings belonging to the Hawkins. Charles knocked on the door. The maid stood behind him to shield herself from the barrage of improprieties to come. Mrs Hawkins answered the door.

'Good day, madam,' said Charles cheerfully.

'Oh, it's you,' grunted Mrs Hawkins. Charles could tell that she was flustered, presumably by the argument with her maid earlier that day. Mrs Hawkins saw her maid cowering behind the short stature of the minister. 'Come you in here now!' she demanded of the maid.

'Now, Mrs Hawkins. Please be calm. I came across your maid after prayers today and saw she was very unhappy. Perhaps you could find it in your heart to forgive the poor girl whatever she has done?'

'I will do no such thing, Mr Wesley!' snapped Mrs Hawkins. 'And what is more, this has nothing to do with you. You should stop meddling in other people's business!'

Charles was not prepared for the scorn that poured forth from the mouth of Mrs Hawkins next. Clearly, she was not going to forgive her maid. She grabbed the girl by the arm and pulled her into the house. Then she slammed the door in Charles' face. He hastily retreated from her doorstep and decided to do some pastoral visitation around the settlement, in search of a kinder welcome.

In the evening Charles went on a mercy mission to Colonel Oglethorpe. During his visitations that afternoon, Charles had met a woman who had little in the way of possessions to help her survive the rigours of a new American settlement. He was going to plead on her behalf for some supplies to assist her daily living.

Oglethorpe was in a foul temper with Charles who had no idea what he had done to warrant such harshness. Perhaps the colonel had a dislike for Charles' rules for Christian living, or maybe it was his preaching. Perhaps Charles was not such a good administrator as Oglethorpe had hoped for. Whatever the reason, it was the first time Charles had experienced Oglethorpe's displeasure, but it wasn't the last. The relationship between them grew sour. Charles could not account for Oglethorpe's coldness. Whatever it was that annoyed him, Charles would remain dignified in his dealings with the colonel.

On Thursday 18th March, Charles went for a walk to clear his head. He was praying as he walked when he heard someone shoot at him from across the bushes. Just at that moment, Charles had turned to walk in a different direction so the bullet whizzed by and did not hit him. He could not understand why someone would want him maimed or even dead! He had only been at the settlement for eleven days. Frederica was proving to be a challenging experience right from the start.

The colonel had banned shooting on Sundays. This was a problem for Dr Hawkins. He had been the surgeon on the *Simmonds*, and now he was the doctor in residence at Frederica. Hawkins had discharged his weapon on Sunday, 21st March. He was arrested for breaking the colonel's orders.

The arrest threw Mrs Hawkins into a fit of rage. She discharged a gun herself and insisted that she should be confined to jail along with her husband. The guards told her to go away which she did reluctantly, swearing an oath to kill the first man that should come near her.

Later that day, Mrs Hawkins ran into Charles talking with a parishioner in the street. Mrs Hawkins was still livid about the events earlier that day. She blamed Charles for her husband's incarceration in the guardroom. Shooting on Sundays was permitted until he came to Frederica. She berated him with bad language and threatened to do him as much harm as she could.

> 'She said she would blow me up, and my brother,' Charles wrote in his diary, 'that she would be revenged, and expose my hypocrisy, my prayers four times a day by beat of drum, and abundance more which I cannot write and thought no woman … could have spoken!'[2]

Although shaken by the exchange, Charles remained calm through it all. He told her that he hoped she would feel better soon. Her true colours were now revealed to him. She was not an ally in his mission to America, as she pretended to be on the *Simmonds*.

Further difficulties came to pass with the colonel. Oglethorpe did not permit Charles his own bed but ordered him to sleep on the floor of another man's hut. As if that wasn't enough, Charles was accused by the colonel of inciting the men of the settlement to mutiny.

2. Charles Wesley's *Journal*, Volume 1, page 5, entry for Sunday, 21 March, 1736.

'Mr Wesley,' called Oglethorpe from outside the minister's hut, 'I would like to speak with you.'

It was seven thirty in the morning. On hearing the colonel's voice, Charles quickly prayed for God's help. He opened the door and stood before Oglethorpe. The colonel appeared somewhat combative, so Charles steeled himself for some direct conversation.

'Good morning, Colonel,' greeted Charles pleasantly. 'What can I do for you?'

'You can begin by putting an end to your troublemaking and mutiny sir!' bellowed Oglethorpe.

'I don't understand,' replied Charles calmly.

'Mr Wesley, it has been brought to my attention that you are stirring up the people to desert the settlement,' continued Oglethorpe. 'There was a meeting last night.'

'A meeting?'

'I received a message from them this morning of their desire to go. The men are constantly at your services, Mr Wesley, and so it is clear to me that you have put them up to this! Let there be no misunderstanding – I shall shoot half-a-dozen of them at once! It is only out of kindness that I have decided to speak to you first!'

It was news to Charles. 'I can assure you, Colonel, that I know nothing about their meeting or their purposes,' he said. 'I never incited anyone to leave Frederica. I would like to face my accuser face to face.'

'It was Lawley,' confirmed Oglethorpe. 'I will fetch him. Wait here.'

'Mr Lawley?' repeated Charles, hardly surprised by the revelation. Mr Lawley was no peacemaker by any stretch of the imagination.

Oglethorpe began to walk away in search of Lawley. 'Let me assure you, Colonel, that I have always, and will continue to make it my business to promote peace among everyone,' said Charles to the back of Oglethorpe's head.

Charles then sought out Ingham to tell him what was going on and to ask him to pray. The two Oxford men went for a walk. It was not long before Oglethorpe and Lawley could be seen approaching. Ingham left as the men reached their position. Oglethorpe took control of the conversation. He spoke of the quarrel the people had with Charles in a general manner. He did not appear to be angry with Charles in front of Lawley. This strategy unnerved Lawley who seemed to be full of guilt and fear. He changed his accusation against Charles from inciting the people to riot, to 'forcing the people to prayers!'

'The people themselves will acquit me of that,' replied Charles to the amended charge. 'I am persuaded that their desire to leave the settlement arose from a mistake, not from malice, Colonel Oglethorpe.'

The colonel looked at Lawley and said, 'Mr Lawley, tell the 'petitioners' (not 'mutineers') that I will not seek out their identities if they remain peaceable in future. I hope they will be so, and Mr Wesley here hopes so too.'

'Yes sir' replied Lawley. 'I really believe it of Mr Wesley, and had always a great respect for him,' he added.

'Yes, you had always a great respect for Mr Wesley. You told me he was a stirrer up of sedition.' Lawley winced at Oglethorpe's mild rebuke. 'You may leave us, Mr Lawley,' said the colonel.

Once Lawley was out of earshot, Charles said, 'Thank you, Colonel, for speaking with me first. I beg you to always do so.'

'I promise I will, Mr Wesley,' replied Oglethorpe. Charles then went to find Ingham. He wanted to tell his colleague how things were settled.

'I fear that this is just the beginning of your sorrows here, Charles,' said Ingham when the story was finished.

Ingham's words could not have been truer. Charles' relationship with Oglethorpe remained strained much to his dismay. He could not work out what it was that kept Oglethorpe cold towards him. The opposition of the settlers to his religious zeal also continued. A distraught Charles persuaded Ingham to go to Savannah and fetch his brother, John, and Delamotte, who were ministering there.

Soon after dispatching Ingham, a battle-weary Charles succumbed to a fever. However, he pressed on with his duties, albeit at a slower pace than before. While he waited for his rescuers to arrive, Charles noticed that those who may have held him in regard were now avoiding him.

That night in his journal, Charles wrote down what he felt,

> 'My few well-wishers are afraid to speak to me. Some have turned out of the way to avoid me. Others desired I would not take it ill if they seemed not to know me when we should meet. The servant that used to wash my linen sent it back unwashed.'[3]

It came to Charles' attention that some wooden boards were marked for destruction. He tried to get a few so that he could lie on them at night instead of sleeping on the ground. His request was refused. Then a man in the settlement died and Charles obtained his bed. He got one good night's sleep on it before Oglethorpe took it away from him. The day it happened, Charles scribbled:

> 'Today Mr Oglethorpe gave away my bedstead from under me and refused to spare one of the carpenters to mend me up another.'[4]

Poor Charles. He never imagined that ministry in America would be so hard. It never occurred to him that his parishioners would reject his loving concern for their souls. 'Perhaps John is having more success in the capital city,' he wondered.

Meanwhile, Ingham arrived in Savannah. He told John and Delamotte of Charles' struggles. Horrified, the men wasted no time in leaving for Frederica. It

---

3. Charles Wesley's *Journal*, Volume 1, page 15, entry for Wednesday, 31 March, 1736.
4. Charles Wesley's *Journal*, Volume 1, page 17, entry for Thursday, 8 April, 1736.

would be a trip of one hundred miles in open canoe along the coast south to St Simon's Island. They arrived in Frederica on Saturday, 10 April.

John discovered Charles desperately ill, lying on the floor of his tent. He was not able to lead services or act in his capacity as Oglethorpe's secretary, so John stepped in to both roles. Oglethorpe was pleased to have John there as his gifting for administration was much greater than his sick brother's.

Eventually the reason for Oglethorpe's displeasure of Charles came out. John discovered that it all came from the evil tongues of Mrs Welsh and Mrs Hawkins. They accused Charles of spreading unfounded rumours of impropriety between the ladies and Oglethorpe. No wonder the colonel was cold towards him.

When John learned of their evil scheme and how it developed, he spoke to Charles and then Oglethorpe and told them what the women had done. The colonel confronted Charles about the rumours. Charles defended himself vigorously and denied any wrongdoing. Oglethorpe was convinced of Charles' sincerity and his old love and confidence in Charles returned.

However, the damage had been done. Charles had been there just under three months when he left, having arranged to swap locations with his brother John.

When he was at Savannah, Charles preached every morning and evening service on Sunday. He visited parishioners during the week. This routine, however, was interrupted by Colonel Oglethorpe when he arrived in Savannah a short time later.

There were rumours going about that the State of Georgia was on the brink of ruin. Oglethorpe wanted to stop these rumours from being spread. He certainly did not want them to be believed by his trustees back in England. So, the colonel had an important job for Charles to do. Charles was to return to England and testify to the board of trustees that the colony was flourishing.

Charles was glad to leave. America was a land of sorrows for him, so he boarded a ship and left Savannah on Monday, 26 July, 1736.

Why did his first charge in ministry fail? Maybe it was because the people rejected his strict rules for holy living. Perhaps he was too sensitive to the attitudes and opinions of the men and women around him. A bit of both perhaps, but Charles was not yet converted. His only message in Frederica was to encourage the people to be full of 'good works' – 'if you do this or that, then God will be pleased with you, and hopefully he will let you into his heaven.'

This was more wishful thinking than true biblical hope in the Lord. Charles was still unaware of his great need to be 'born again' in Christ.[5]

---

5. John 3:1-17; 1 Peter 1:3-5.

Chaplain in Savannah

During the time that Charles and Ingham left the *Simmonds* for Frederica, John and Delamotte remained in Savannah. The town of Savannah lay by the bank of a wide river and acted as the main port for the State of Georgia. The first settlers of 1732 had built wooden houses of a similar size and design. When John arrived in 1736, a further 150 homes were added by the new settlers. Some of these new homes were two or three stories high. The houses were painted giving an air of comfort and sophistication to the town. The Court House doubled up as the building in which the church met each week for services.

The minister whom John was replacing was still living in the wooden parsonage, so for the first three weeks of their arrival in America, John and Delamotte lived on board the *Simmonds*.

During that time the Oxford men received a visit from the chief of the native Yamacraw Indians. He was called Tomo Chachi. A couple of years earlier Tomo

Chachi had travelled with his nephew and Oglethorpe to England, to meet the trustees of the new State of Georgia. It was an indication to the trustees in England that Oglethorpe's work in Georgia was successful and therefore worthwhile.

Tomo Chachi walked up the gangplank and stepped on board the deck of the *Simmonds*. He was accompanied by his wife, his nephew, two other women and a few children. An interpreter called Mrs Musgrove took up the rear. The ship's captain greeted the boarding party and led them to his large cabin. They waited momentarily until the Oxford missionaries came in to meet them. They greeted each other warmly.

'I am glad you are come,' said Tomo Chachi through the interpreter, Mrs Musgrove. 'When I was in England, I desired that some would speak the great Word to me. And my nation then desired to hear it.'

John smiled. Oh how he loved to hear of people desiring the Word of God!

'We are all in confusion, so I am glad that you have come,' said the chief. 'I will go up and speak to the wise men of our nation. And I hope they will listen to me.' Tomo Chachi looked solemnly at the men and said in a grave tone, 'But we would not be made Christians as the Spaniards make Christians. We would be taught the Word first, before we are baptised.'

'There is but One, He that sits in heaven, who is able to teach man wisdom,' replied John through the interpreter. 'Though we have come so far to be here, we do not know whether He will be pleased to teach you by us or not. If He teaches you, you will learn wisdom, but we can do nothing without Him.'

Tomo Chachi was pleased enough with the response. It was a short meeting. The Oxford missionaries left the room, and the boarding party left the *Simmonds*. John really hoped that God had a great work for him to do among the Indians in Georgia.

After three weeks lodging at the *Simmonds*, John and Delamotte moved their belongings to stay with the Moravians in their settlement until the parsonage was free. On the first Sunday in March, John preached to a large congregation who had come out to hear him. The townsfolk listened attentively to their new pastor. John seemed to have awakened an interest in spiritual things within them. At the same time, Delamotte started a good work with the children of the town. They moved into the parsonage on Monday, 15 March.

All in all, there were about seven hundred people under their pastoral care. The work had begun well although it was interrupted by a visit from Ingham. He told John and Delamotte of all the terrible things that Charles had endured since he arrived in Frederica. The folks there had told Oglethorpe all manner of lies about Charles. The colonel believed them, and decided to deal severely with Charles.

'He is denied even the most common comforts,' Ingham reported. 'I fear that his life is in jeopardy through the malice of his enemies,' he added.

John and Delamotte made haste to be with Charles. They left Ingham in charge of the church and school in Savannah while they were away. It was only a short time before they were back in Savannah and Ingham returned to Frederica. There was no doubt that John's presence in Frederica went some way to relieving the tension that Charles was experiencing there. But the men believed that Frederica was a spiritually barren place.

John worked in Frederica for two short stints during 1736 – with little success. John found that the people were doggedly persistent to hinder the work of ministry. Those Fredericans who had a more agreeable manner towards him could scarce show their true feelings for fear of angering his opponents.

John's final stay in Frederica was in January 1737. Delamotte was with him. They did not receive a warm welcome from the settlers. John wrote in his journal:

> 'After having beaten the air in this unhappy place for twenty days, on January 26th I took my final leave of Frederica. It was not my apprehension of my own danger, though my life had been threatened many times, but an utter despair of doing good there, which made me content with the thought of seeing it no more.'[1]

Returning to Savannah, John and Delamotte got stuck into work once more. It was customary for John to write reports for the trustees and supporters back in England. In one report, John told them about

---

1. John Wesley's *Journal*, Volume 1, page 44, entry for Saturday, 1 January, 1737. John comments on arriving in Frederica on 5, January, 1737.

their work with children. They taught the children their 'catechism', which was a text that contained the Apostles Creed, the Lord's Prayer, and the Ten Commandments. The catechism was used to teach the children how to follow the Lord Jesus in their daily lives.

After a year of ministry, Delamotte was teaching between thirty and forty children how to read, write and do sums as well. The weekly timetable was full. Before school in the morning and when school was finished in the afternoon, he spent time catechising the younger children. In the evenings he instructed the older children.

Every Saturday afternoon and Sunday before the evening service, John got involved with the children and he spent time catechising all of them. Every week during the Sunday service a select number of the children would repeat something that they had learned from catechism class. John would then go on to explain in greater detail what the children recited to the congregation.

After the evening service every Sunday, some parishioners would meet at John's house for a time of prayer and singing hymns (probably hymns that he and his brother Charles wrote, as this was also a great gifting they had). A smaller number of people would meet at the parsonage on Saturday evenings for the same purpose.

America was full of work for the Oxford missionaries. However, the mission to the Indians did not turn out as John had hoped. As he was the minister to the people of Savannah, he had little time to meet the Indian nations. When he managed to arrange some time with them, they said they were too busy fighting wars to learn the gospel of Christ. Perhaps later when the wars were over, they told him.

Ingham had left for England in February 1737 to enlist the help of others for the mission in America. Among his letters was one written by John to George Whitefield, imploring him to come over. 'The harvest is so great and the labourers so few. What if you are the man, Mr Whitefield?' he wrote.

By the summer that year, the good work that was achieved in Georgia was under threat. During his time there, John had met a young woman called Sophia Hopkey. She was the niece of Mr Causton who was the storekeeper and the local magistrate of Savannah. John liked Sophia very much. Sophia was fond of him too and it looked for a moment that they might get married. But John took too long to ask for her hand in marriage. Tired of waiting, Sophia turned her attentions to another colonist called William Williamson. Although she told John that she had no intention of marrying Williamson because he was just a friend, she did marry him without John's knowledge.

When John found out, he was annoyed. He stopped her taking communion at a service one Sunday morning because he believed her to be a liar and not in a fit state to receive the sacrament.[2] Mortified, Sophia told her new husband, Mr Williamson, who decided to sue John for defamation of character.

In his capacity as the local magistrate, Mr Causton arranged a large jury that would convict John of any offence levelled against him. A number of other false accusations were charged against him – things he allegedly said and did to cause further offence.

It was clear to John that no matter what he argued in his defence, he would not be listened to. His mission to the Indians, the main reason he agreed to be in Georgia, never truly came to pass. Perhaps it was time to leave America?

John decided it was time to leave Georgia. On 4 November, 1737, John made this intention clear to the townsfolk of Savannah by pinning a notice to the church door. He would leave the town in four weeks. The magistrate, Mr Causton, ordered that John should be prevented from leaving Savannah and declared it was forbidden for anyone to help him.

As soon as evening prayers were over, on Friday, 2 December, John made his escape from Georgia. He travelled by boat with three friends to South Carolina, heading to England. His friend and fellow-worker Charles Delamotte remained in Savannah.

It took ten days for John to reach Charlestown, partly because his little group got lost in the dense woods of the American landscape, where they

2. 1 Corinthians 11:23-29.

suffered greatly from cold and hunger. But on 22 December he boarded the *Samuel*, a ship bound for England.

The journey home gave John time to reflect on his mission to Georgia. He was convinced that he had no faith in Christ and this prevented his heart from being troubled and afraid. In his opinion, if he truly believed in God he would not feel this way. He was troubled by the fear of death. He had shown his faith by his good works, giving to the poor and other charitable actions. But when the storms arose at sea, he felt the storms of doubt and lack of faith within. He began to doubt that he was truly right with God. In fact, he wondered if the gospel was true at all. 'What if the gospel wasn't true? Have I suffered in vain? Has it all been for nothing?' he thought.

'I went to America to convert the Indians, but O! Who shall convert me?!' he wrote in his journal. 'Who, is he that will deliver me from this evil heart of unbelief?'[3]

This was the torment that John felt deep inside his heart, especially when confronted with his own mortality. Death terrified him.

Towards the end of his voyage to England, John sat at a small table in his cabin during a period of calm weather, and penned a summary of the lessons he learned in Georgia.

'It is now two years and almost four months since I left my native country, in order to teach the Georgian Indians

---

3. John Wesley's *Journal*, Volume 1, page 74, entry for Tuesday, 24 January, 1738.

the nature of Christianity. But what have I learned myself in the meantime?'

John lifted his quill from the paper. He thought for a moment before resuming his writing, then continued.

'Why, (what I the least of all suspected,) that I who went to America to convert others, was never myself converted to God ... the faith I want is a "sure trust and confidence in God, that, through the merits of Jesus Christ, my sins are forgiven, and I reconciled to the favour of God."'[4]

John was back in England by 1 February, 1738. Although he was feeling despondent, he wanted with all his heart to find that faith which would deliver him from fear and doubt and bring assurance of God's acceptance to his soul.

The blessing of God that he longed for was near at hand.

---

4. John Wesley's *Journal*, Volume 1, page 75, entry for Sunday, 29 January, 1738.

My Chains Fell Off

Returning one night from pastoral duties in Wapping, England, George Whitefield found three letters from Georgia in America. Charles and John had written to him. They did not sound so happy in their correspondence. However, the content of the letters fired George's imagination. In his mind's eye, he saw himself preaching to the Native Americans, telling them about the saving gospel of Christ Jesus.

George knew about the young state of Georgia that had been established by James Oglethorpe, a charitable venture to help debtors from England gain a fresh start rather than rotting in prison. He knew of the persecuted German protestants who fled to Georgia along with some other folks from Britain, to tame the wild and unexplored country of America, and to form a buffer against the Spaniards who edged up from Florida towards the north.

For the moment, George put the idea of Georgia behind him and focused his efforts on the Methodist Society that was established in Oxford.

Soon after another letter arrived from John Wesley. In it he made a personal plea to George. 'The harvest is so great and the labourers so few. What if you are the man, Mr Whitefield?'

Charles arrived back from America in the middle of December 1736. He wrote a letter to George, and told him, 'The master calls – arise, obey.'

George answered that he would set sail for Georgia as soon as possible. A year later, he received his sailing orders to join the ship called the *Whitaker*, in the lower Thames in London. He was invited to preach in Upper Deal church while the voyagers who were heading to America waited for a suitable wind to blow them out to sea and on their way.

While George preached in Upper Deal, the news came that John Wesley had arrived in England. George was excited that he might see his old friend and mentor before he set sail. But word came that he had already left for London.

John was aware that George had not yet departed due to the unpredictable winds around the port. As he had now returned to England, John prayed for his friend as to whether George should stay or go. John cast lots, and he enclosed the outcome via a messenger. He had written on a small note, 'Let him return to London.'

For a brief moment, George did not know what to do. He felt hurt that his old friend and mentor left the port at Upper Deal in a hurry and did not make the effort to see him face to face. But he could not return to London and renege on his word to serve the Master in Georgia. He wrote a kind but firm refusal to John and sailed for America the following day.

Charles did not realise that John had returned from the mission field in Georgia until he was actually back in England. He was staying at the home of Mr Hutton, a bookseller with a store near Drury Lane in London, when John appeared at the door that night. It was a wonderful shock to Charles to be reunited with his brother once more. Mr Hutton was pleased to have John stay with them too.

During the weeks that followed, John threw himself into a hectic round of engagements. Charles had done a similar thing when he returned from America fourteen months earlier. John was asked to give an account of the colony in America, which he did without hesitation. They wanted to know why he left Georgia, so he told them candidly of his experience there.

It was his pleasure to preach in various places around London as well. John always prayed that what he said to his congregations was not in vain. He and his brother, Charles, preached the importance of living upright lives and doing good works. With all their strength they encouraged people to lead a religious life and to pray more. They even begged people to flee from the wrath of God to come,[1] but they never told people where to flee to! This was soon to change.

---

1. 1 Thessalonians 1:10.

On Tuesday, 7 February, while visiting a friend in London, John and Charles met a young Moravian called Peter Böhler. Peter was passing through London with a couple of friends on their way to America. He was going to be a missionary to the African slaves in Carolina. It was quickly discovered that Peter did not know how to speak English, but knew Latin. As the Wesley brothers were also fluent in Latin, it was the language used to converse with their new friend.

As soon as John discovered that his young German friends had no acquaintances in England, he offered to get them some lodging near Mr Hutton's place. John and Charles were resolved to spend as much time as possible with them while they were in London. By the middle of February, however, Peter, John and Charles travelled to Oxford.

Often, they talked to each other about the gospel of Jesus Christ. 'True faith in Jesus resulted in power over sin and constant peace from a sense of forgiveness,' Peter contended.

Amazed by this revelation, John exclaimed, 'If this is so, I have not faith!' With all his might John tried to impress upon his Moravian friend his firm belief that forgiveness of sins and peace with God needed to be earned by ongoing effort. Peter was astonished to hear this and said to John, 'My brother, my brother, that philosophy of yours must be purged away!'

John didn't understand what he meant. Peter pressed him more. 'Believe and you will be saved,' he said. 'Believe in the Lord Jesus with all your heart and nothing shall be impossible to you! This faith, like the salvation it brings, is the *free gift of God*. Seek and you will find. Strip yourself bare of your own good works and self-righteousness and lay yourself before him! For everyone that comes to Jesus, he will in no wise cast out.'

Soon after, John left for London. Remaining in Oxford, Peter had the opportunity to speak to Charles on his own about his faith in Jesus. One evening towards the end of February, Charles was feeling dreadfully unwell. His suffering was so bad that he thought he was going to die. Peter came to his bedside late at night.

'Will you pray with me?' asked Charles weakly. Peter began to pray softly at first, but as he continued, his voice got louder. He prayed for Charles' full recovery from his illness.

Then Peter took his ailing friend's hand. 'You will not die now,' he said.

Charles was unsure if he could last until the morning as the pain was so severe, but if he did, he thought he would recover indeed.

'Do you hope to be saved?' asked Peter.

'Yes.'

'For what reason do you hope it?'

Charles thought for a moment. 'Because I have used my best endeavours to serve God,' he replied.

Peter shook his head negatively and remained silent. Charles thought his friend was being most uncharitable. 'What, are my endeavours not a sufficient ground of

71

hope?' he thought to himself. 'I have nothing else to trust to.'

By the morning, Charles was moderately better and on Saturday, 4 March John arrived at Charles' lodgings and Peter was there with him.

Since his conversation with Peter about salvation in Christ alone, John had spent time in the Scriptures and in prayer. On Sunday, 5 March, the day after arriving in Oxford, he suddenly realised that Peter was right. For the first time in his life, John was now convinced of his lack of faith in Christ's saving power on the cross.

'Peter, I must ask you, should I leave off preaching to others, as I have not faith myself?' asked John.

'By no means,' answered Peter.

'But what can I preach?' asked John.

'Preach faith till you have it. And then, because you have it, you will preach faith,' Peter replied.

The very next day John had the chance to preach the 'new' doctrine of salvation by faith alone in Christ alone. He visited the prison in Oxford and spoke to a prisoner under the death sentence. His name was Clifford. On a number of occasions Peter Böhler had asked John to speak with Clifford, but it was only now that John had opportunity to do so. He followed up this meeting with Clifford later on in March, on the very day that Clifford was to be hanged – Monday, 27 March, 1738. On his pastoral visit of the condemned man, John was accompanied by a friend. That evening, John sat with his journal open in front of him. He began to record carefully what had happened that day.

> 'We prayed with the condemned man ... in such words as were given us in that hour. Clifford kneeled down in much heaviness and confusion, having no rest in his bones, by reason of his sins. After a time, he rose up, and eagerly said, "I am now ready to die. I know Christ has taken away my sins and there is no more condemnation for me." In his last moments he was enjoying a perfect peace, in confidence that he was "accepted in the Beloved."'[2]

A few weeks later, John was challenged once again by Peter Böhler who was still in England. Peter claimed that faith could come instantaneously.

'The worst sinner could receive immediate salvation if they repented of their sins and trusted in Christ alone,' asserted Peter.

John was stunned. He had not heard of such a thing. He had personally not experienced this immediate conversion.

'How can a man at once be turned from darkness to light?' queried John. 'How is it possible that he can be turned from sin and misery to righteousness and joy in the Holy Spirit?'

John searched the Scriptures and especially the book of Acts in the New Testament.[3] To his astonishment he discovered that he could hardly find any conversion that wasn't instantaneous.

---

2. John Wesley's *Journal*, Volume 1, page 90, entry for Monday, 27 March, 1738.

3. To find out more, read *Adventures in Acts*, and *More Adventures in Acts* by the author, published by Christian Focus Publications.

The next day was a Sunday. In the evening, Peter arrived with three men to see John. They testified that God had given them in a moment such a faith in the blood of his Son, and that God had transformed them from darkness into light, and out of sin and fear into holiness and happiness. John confessed that he could no longer raise any objection. All he could do was cry out, 'Lord, please help me in my unbelief!' He then asked Peter, 'Should I not refrain from teaching others?'

'No,' said Peter confidently. 'Do not hide the talent God has given you, John.'

On the way back to his lodgings, Peter was discussing the evening's events with his friends.

'You are very fond of Mr Wesley,' asked one of them.

'Yes I am. He is a poor sinner, who has a broken heart. He hungers after a better righteousness than that which he has had up till now. His hunger is for a righteousness which is in the blood of Jesus Christ.'

When John finally had a chance to catch up with Charles a couple of days later, he spoke about this new understanding of conversion. Charles became cross with John. He did not like his brother John's determination to proclaim such a view, because it was offensive in polite society among those who tried to do good, in order to obtain God's pleasure.

However, this was an issue that Charles would have to come back to, sooner than he realised. During the last weekend in April, Charles began to be ill again with pleurisy[4]. He was back in London at Hutton's place and went straight to bed when he arrived. In the morning Charles received an unexpected visit from Peter Böhler who had been held back from his trip to Carolina in America.

Peter stood at the bedside of his sick friend and prayed for him. Charles was moved by Peter's kindness and wondered if he ought to consider Peter's doctrine of faith. Perhaps he should examine for himself if he really did have saving faith in Christ. If not, he would never stop looking and longing for it until he had it.

Finally Peter Böhler left London on 4 May in order to embark for Carolina in America.

'O what a work has God begun since his coming into England!'[5] was the entry in John's journal for that day.

Charles thought he might move on to the home of Mr Sutton senior, who lived in Westminster. But then a visit by an English Moravian called John Bray, changed his mind. Charles was invited to stay with Mr Bray while he recuperated, and he agreed.

At first, Charles though Mr Bray was just an ignorant mechanic who didn't know much about anything. However, Mr Bray knew Jesus Christ personally and Charles believed that God had placed Mr Bray in his life for a reason – to help him find that saving faith in Christ that he was searching for.

---

4. *Pleurisy* is an illness that infects the lungs and causes sharp pains in the chest.

5. John Wesley's *Journal*, Volume 1, page 93, entry for Thursday, 4 May, 1738.

Over the following nine days Charles felt worse than ever. Mr Bray read the Scriptures and prayed with his sick friend. It brought a lot of comfort to Charles. Shortly after, another friend called in to see Charles. He gave him a copy of a book written by Martin Luther on the New Testament letter of Galatians.

As Charles read Luther's insights about 'Justification by faith' his own views were transformed. He was especially struck by Galatians 2:20: 'The Son of God who loved me, and gave himself to die for me.'

On Sunday, 21 May, 1738, Charles was visited by his brother John and a group of his friends. They sang a hymn together and prayed. It was a short visit. When John and the men left, Charles settled down to sleep. As he was drifting off he heard a voice outside his door, although in his drowsiness he thought the voice came from within the room. It was Mr Bray's sister who was determined to help Charles through his spiritual ordeal.

Her courage failed her to enter the room. So, she stood outside the door and in a loud voice said, 'In the name of Jesus of Nazareth, arise, and believe, and you shall be healed of all your infirmities.'

Suddenly all the uncertainty and confusion of the previous weeks were swept away as he grasped hold of that assurance of faith which he had been looking for. He opened his Bible and read from Psalm 40. 'He put a new song in my mouth, a song of praise to our God. Many will see and fear, and put their trust in the Lord' (Psalm 40:3).

Before he slept that night, he wrote in his journal, 'I now found myself at peace with God, and rejoiced in hope of loving Christ . . . I saw that by faith I stood!'[6]

Two days later Charles started to write a new song to celebrate his conversion.[7] He showed the half-written song to Mr Bray who encouraged Charles to finish it.

Meanwhile, John was still unfulfilled in his search for assurance of faith. On the evening of Wednesday, 24 May, John went grudgingly with a friend to a Moravian meeting in Nettleton Court just off Aldersgate Street in the City of London. He wasn't in the mood to be there, but now that he was, he might as well pay attention to what was being said. John listened to someone read Martin Luther's 'Preface' to his book on the New Testament letter to the Romans.

And then it happened! A miracle! John wrote in his journal.

> 'A quarter before nine, while the speaker was describing the change which God works in the heart through faith in Christ, I felt my heart strangely warmed ... I felt I did trust in Christ, Christ alone for salvation; and an assurance was given to me that he had taken away my sins, even mine, and saved me from the law of sin and death.'[8]

The meeting in Aldersgate Street was not far away from where Charles was staying. Just before ten that

---

6. Charles Wesley's *Journal*, Volume 1, page 92, entry for Sunday, 21 May, 1738.
7. See the *Fact File* called 'Hymns and Poems' in the back of the book.
8. John Wesley's *Journal*, Volume 1, page 103, entry for Monday, 22 – Wednesday, 24 May, 1738.

night, John arrived with a group of friends. When he saw Charles, John triumphantly exclaimed, 'I believe! I believe!' Although John did not like physical contact much, Charles hugged him.

'We must sing praise to God!' said Charles. 'Look here, brother, I have written a new song,' he said excitedly as he held up the musical manuscript.

'Let's sing it then!' exclaimed John. 'Let me see the words.' He held out his hand and Charles handed him the music. John began to read.

'I like this verse very much,' John said, encouraging his brother immensely. 'Yes, yes, "my chains fell off, my heart was free!"' he exclaimed. 'Such wonderful words.' He continued reading, '"No condemnation now I dread, Jesus and all in him is mine!" Oh my dearest brother Charles. Splendid. Lead us in this new song!'

The men sang the new hymn with joy and exuberance. Then they prayed together, before John and his friends left Charles in peace. They had almost forgotten he wasn't well and needed his rest to get better. It was time for them to go and for Charles to sleep.

Preaching Outdoors

George Whitefield returned to London after a brief stay in Georgia. He wanted to raise funds for an orphanage there, and to be ordained as a priest in the Church of England. It took eleven weeks for his boat to cross the Atlantic to England. Violent storms kept causing the ship to be blown off course and he was forced to land in Ireland. However, eventually George arrived on the shores of England on 8 December, 1738, not knowing anything about the Wesleys' newfound faith.

By now, Charles and John were preaching the new truths they had learned, in the prisons and pulpits of London. It was not long before each discovered that a faithful and passionate proclamation of the gospel was rarely given a second invite into an Anglican pulpit.

Earlier in the year, John had started a religious society in the Moravian Chapel in Fetter Lane in London. Those who gathered wanted to meet every week in order to pray for one another. So, when James Hutton met George and took him to his home near Drury Lane, they wasted no time before heading out to the Fetter Lane society. George received an enthusiastic welcome when he appeared at that meeting.

Knowing that George was coming back to England, Hutton tried in earnest to secure some preaching engagements for him in local pulpits. He found that the churches of London were not that happy to hear of George's return. He was a known accomplice of John and Charles Wesley, both of whom had already been locked out of London pulpits. There were, however, some churches who were pleased to welcome George.

John and Charles were in Oxford when news of George's arrival from America reached them. They hurried back to London to see him and called at Hutton's home. The former members of the Holy Club spent a wonderful evening catching up with each other. It was an emotional reunion. There was so much to tell each other that they didn't stop talking until after midnight.

From that time up to Christmas, the men found their diaries full of preaching engagements. In the New Year, George made a quick visit to Oxford to be ordained by his old mentor, Dr Martin Benson, who was the Bishop of Gloucester. When George returned to London he preached to a huge congregation in south London. There were over a thousand people unable to get in to hear him. They stood outside in the graveyard hoping to hear something of his sermon. He wondered if he might preach to them in the graveyard afterwards, but was quite reticent to do that in case he offended the clergy or anyone else in attendance.

George left London and headed west to Bristol, stopping at a couple of other places on the way, to raise funds for the orphanage back in Georgia. He found the pulpits were closed to him due to his 'enthusiasm' for the gospel of Jesus. There was nothing else for it – he would preach in the open air.

He was not far from where the Kingswood colliers worked. Unfortunately, the colliers had a bad reputation for being violent and illiterate. This did not deter George from bringing them the gospel.

George was dressed in a long black cassock, and a gown. He wore preaching bands around his neck, commonly worn by clergy. He stood on a raised piece of land. When the coal miners were leaving the pits, he announced his text from Matthew's Gospel in a loud and clear voice.

'Blessed are the poor in spirit,' he proclaimed loudly, 'for they shall see the kingdom of heaven.'

A small group of minors stopped and looked at him. 'Matthew, chapter five and verses one to three,' continued George. Then he cracked a joke. A few more miners stopped and gathered around. He began to preach the gospel. Much to his surprise, they listened intently. And when George had finished his sermon, at least two hundred miners were standing around him. Some of the hardened men were in tears, having been moved by the Word of God.

A bowling green in the heart of the city was one of the open spaces set aside for George's services. Soon there were congregations numbering ten to twenty thousand people who were clamouring to hear the gospel from George. The spiritual harvest in England was ripe for the picking.

For six weeks George continued this work. As successful as his ministry was in Bristol, George planned to return to Georgia. He invited John to leave London and take his place in Bristol. John was busy, but decided to accept his friend's offer, at least to see for himself what George had been doing all this time. Charles felt that if John accepted the invitation his brother would be going to a certain death! At times Charles could be a bit overdramatic especially if he was ignorant of a work that he hadn't heard of before.

John was unsure about open-air preaching. The 'Conventicle Act'[1] prohibited open-air preaching except at a public hanging.

In the evening of Saturday, 31 March, 1739, John arrived in Bristol and met George. The following day was Sunday. John stood in the middle of George's huge congregation. He found it difficult to think about preaching in the open fields. He had always felt that the saving of souls should be confined to a church building, and it was almost a sin if it happened anywhere else.

By the end of the day George had said his farewells to his congregations and had headed off to London. John

---

1. A *conventicle* was an unlawful assembly of 'worship' in places other than Anglican churches. For more information about *The Conventicle Act*, see *Fact File* at the back of the book.

spent that evening with a little society in Nicholas Street preaching on a passage from the 'Sermon on the Mount'.

The next day, at four o'clock in the afternoon, John stood on a small piece of raised ground in a brickfield just outside the city. He preached to about three thousand people on the Bible verse from Luke's Gospel, 'The Spirit of the Lord is upon me, because he has anointed me to proclaim good news to the poor. He has sent me to proclaim liberty to the captives and recovering of sight to the blind, to set at liberty those who are oppressed, to proclaim the year of the Lord's favor.'[2]

This was the first of many gatherings over the next ten weeks of uninterrupted preaching and teaching. At first John drew smaller crowds. He had quite a different style of preaching to George Whitefield. George was full of grand gestures and eloquent words. He was passionate and emotional. John on the other hand was plain and logical, but effective.

He soon organised a regular, methodical schedule of meetings throughout the week all over Bristol city. Every other Tuesday, John would visit the city of Bath twelve miles east of Bristol, and preach there.

The work prospered and on 12 May, 1739, the foundation stone was laid for the first Methodist meeting room on a piece of land in the Horse Fair area, right in the heart of Bristol. It was an opportunity for the two small Methodist societies of the city to be brought together under one roof. It was to be the

2. Luke 4:18-19

first of many Methodist chapels, or meeting houses, that would spring up all over the country, all thanks to John's incredible ability to organise and develop them.

Charles made his first attempt at outdoor preaching while visiting a place in the countryside just outside London on 29 May. In his journal, Charles wrote:

> 'Franklyn, a farmer, invited me to preach in his field. I did so, to about five hundred, on "Repent, for the kingdom of heaven is at hand."'[3]
>
> 'I returned to the house rejoicing.'[4]

Yet on his return to London, Charles was not ready to undertake a regular open-air preaching ministry. George Whitefield tried to persuade Charles to get stuck in despite his reticence. George had been preaching in a park called Moorfields, and on Kennington Common in Lambeth, south London. Huge crowds gathered to hear him preach the gospel. But he was going back to Georgia. Who would take over and preach the gospel to the large numbers of souls thirsting after living waters in these places?

Meanwhile on one of John's regular visits to Bath, the rumoured appearance of a man called Richard 'Beau' Nash at one of John's meetings was causing a commotion. Mr Nash was a celebrated citizen of Bath, with a reputation for being the leader of fashion in eighteenth century Britain. He was influential and well known for scoffing at religion, so much so that John was implored by his supporters not

---

3. Matthew 3:2.
4. Charles Wesley's *Journal*, Volume 1, page 150, entry for Tuesday, 29 May, 1739.

to preach that Tuesday. It was impossible for anyone to predict what might happen if Mr Nash turned up.

John arrived in Bath to discover that his regular congregation had swollen in number. There were many rich and prominent people who had come to see a lively debate between Mr Wesley and Mr Nash.

The meeting began with John telling the gathered throng that they were all sinners. It did not matter if they were rich or poor, or if they were influential or inconsequential in the eyes of society. They were all sinners.

Many seemed surprised and were beginning to think seriously about his message. Sadly, their spiritual conviction was interrupted when Mr Nash arrived at the back of the room. He was dressed as flamboyantly as John was sombrely in his dark cassock and gown.

Mr Nash made his way to the front of the crowd, before sizing up his foe with a condescending snarl on his lip.

'Who gave you the authority to gather these people and preach to them?' demanded Mr Nash, without introducing himself to John.

'By the authority of Jesus Christ, conveyed to me by the Archbishop of Canterbury, when he laid hands upon me, and said, "Take thou authority to preach the gospel,"' answered John in a clear and strong voice.

'This is contrary to an Act of Parliament,' declared Mr Nash. 'This is a conventicle.'

'Sir, the conventicles mentioned in that Act are concerned about seditious meetings. But this meeting is not. There is no shadow of sedition here. Therefore, it is not contrary to the Act.'

Mr Nash paused. The crowd was hanging on every word. What would he say next? Something profound perhaps? Something wise and full of learning perhaps?

'I say it is,' was the deflated response. 'And, besides, your preaching frightens people out of their wits,' said Mr Nash dandily waving a handkerchief between his fingers.

His reply was more comical than profound.

'Sir, did you ever hear me preach?' asked John.

Mr Nash looked at the crowd around him and then awkwardly admitted, 'No.' A few sniggers were heard from the audience.

'How then can you judge what you have never heard?' wondered John.

'Sir, by common report,' said Mr Nash, thinking he was back in the game.

'Common report is not enough,' said John. 'Give me leave, sir, to ask, is not your name Nash?'

'My name is Nash.'

'Sir, I dare not judge you by common report. I do not think it is not enough to judge you in that way.'

Mr Nash paused for a moment to gather his thoughts. Then came the demand. 'I desire to know why these people have come here?'

Before John could say anything else, an elderly lady standing nearby piped up, 'Sir, leave him to me. Let an old woman answer him.' She looked Mr Nash straight in the eye and said, 'You, Mr Nash, take care of your body. We take care of our souls. And for the food of our souls we come here.'

Beau Nash quickly turned and walked away. He walked through the silent crowd, without saying another word, leaving John to resume his meeting in peace. Some thought it a victory for John, but he didn't see it that way. For him, it was another soul remaining lost to the Great Shepherd.[5]

When Mr Nash was gone, John called the people to prayer. He prayed for Mr 'Beau' Nash and for all who opposed the gospel of Christ.

---

5. Isaiah 40:10-11; Ezekiel 34:12; John 10:11-16.

In the Mission Field

The society at Fetter Lane in London was in great confusion. They needed John's wisdom. Letters were sent to him while he was in Bristol requesting his immediate presence back in London to help them.

Ms Lavington, a famous 'prophetess' from France, had infiltrated the membership at Fetter Lane and was causing a stir. She professed to being inspired by God and claimed she had the ability to command Christ to come to her in any shape she wanted – a dove, or an eagle for example. During meetings she would roar out loud when Charles was praying so that no one could hear him. Charles was vexed at her brazenness. She had pulled the wool over some people's eyes, despite his firm warnings about her false claims and teachings.

John arrived in London on 13 June and addressed the congregation about the turmoil Ms Lavington was causing.

'Do not believe every spirit, but test the spirits to see whether they are from God,'[1] John advised them.

---

1. 1 John 4:1

He warned them against false teachers and their lies. He exhorted them to keep true to the gospel. He left the meeting believing that God had removed many of the misunderstandings that had crept in to the society.

Although he was only in London for five days, that Sunday John preached to a large congregation at Moorfields and to an even larger number of people on Kennington Common.

The following Sunday, Charles followed in his brother's footsteps to preach in the open air. His curacy at St Mary's Islington was not going well. He was working with Rev. John Stonehouse who was the rector there. Stonehouse was a friend to both the Wesley brothers and also to Whitefield. The congregation did not care much for the gospel message these men preached.

One of the churchwardens took it upon himself to hound Charles when he was preaching. He accused Charles of not having a licence from the bishop to preach in the Diocese. On two occasions the churchwardens stopped Charles from entering the pulpit! The Bishop of London upheld the complaint of the churchwardens and Charles' ministry in St Mary's came to an end.

George Whitefield suggested to Charles that he needed to minister to another congregation, and could he look after Moorfields on Sunday, 24 June? Charles wrote in his journal:

> 'I prayed and went forth in the name of Jesus Christ. I found near ten thousand helpless sinners waiting for the word [of God] in Moorfields. I invited them in my Master's words, "Come unto me, all you that travail, and are heavy

laden, and I will give you rest."[2] The Lord was with me, even me, his meanest messenger, according to his promise … My load was gone.'[3]

The three friends were now enlisted in this vital open air work for God. Church pulpits across the nation were closed to them, but no one could rob them of large congregations.

By November that year the Wesleys began to preach at the old Foundery in Moorfields. It was a place where cast iron cannons were made for the army. In 1716, an explosion there had led to the removal of the Royal Arsenal to Woolwich on the south bank of the River Thames in London. Only the old buildings were left.

Once John had secured the lease for the property, the Methodists renovated the buildings. They extended the chapel so that it could seat fifteen hundred people. There was a meeting room in which Bible classes were held. One end of this room was fitted out to be a school room, and the other end was turned into a book room where people could buy the many books and pamphlets that the Methodists would publish for sale.

Above the meeting room were John's apartments. His mother Susanna moved in there when the rooms were complete. At the end of the chapel there was a house for the Methodist lay preachers who were trained up for itinerant ministry throughout the nation. A coach house and stable was on site too.

---

2. Matthew 11:28.
3. Charles Wesley's *Journal*, Volume 1, page 155, entry for Sunday, 24 June, 1739.

In those early years, the Foundery became the headquarters for John and Charles' itinerant ministry. In fact, the Methodist movement was mostly confined to London and Bristol. In 1742, however, John decided to make a trip to Newcastle-Upon-Tyne in the north-eastern part of England.

As he walked through the town, John was surprised to see just how many people were drunk from consuming too much alcohol. Not only that, he had never heard so much cursing and swearing, even from the mouths of children! John had never experienced anything like it.

Travelling through the city, John thought to himself, 'Surely this place is ripe for God, who came not to call the righteous but sinners to repentance.'[4]

On his first Sunday preaching there, the size of the congregation was greater than those of Moorfields in London. It was remarkable considering his first observations of the place. Nonetheless, John received a warm welcome from the people of Newcastle. From that moment on, John and Charles were regular visitors to that great English city.

In time, they were able to open 'The Orphan House' as it was known, just outside the town walls. The building was never used as an orphanage, it was just its name. But 'The Orphan House' became the local headquarters for Methodism in the north of England.

---

4. Luke 5:32.

As John was coming back from his first visit to Newcastle, he stopped off at Epworth, his childhood home. When he arrived in any town or city, it was his custom to ask the local clergy if he might preach in their churches. At Epworth, his request was flatly denied.

After the service, one of the locals announced to the departing crowd, 'As Mr Wesley was not being permitted to preach in the church, he has designs to preach here in the graveyard at six o'clock this evening!'

The announcement caused quite a commotion. At six o'clock, John stepped on to his father's tombstone and used it as a platform. He had never seen such a large crowd gathered to hear the gospel in Epworth as he did that night.

John found himself in great demand from the neighbouring villages who wanted him to come and to speak to them. So, he preached to them too. His last sermon in Epworth lasted nearly three hours, and the people hung on his every word. When he was finished, they did not want to let John go. But he needed to return to the Foundery in London.

The Epworth visit made John think about his father. John penned an encouragement to persevere in the Lord's work, in his journal.

> 'Oh, let none think his labour of love is lost because the fruit does not immediately appear. Nearly forty years did my father labour in Epworth, but he saw little fruit of his labour...but the seed sown so long since now sprung up, bringing forth repentance and remission of sins!'[5]

5. John Wesley's *Journal*, Volume 1, page 379, entry for Sunday, 13 June, 1742.

This was the joyful news that John returned to London with. He visited his mother, Susanna, who was now living in the Foundery. She was most unwell, but news of Epworth cheered her heart.

Susanna Wesley died on 23 July, 1742. Charles was out of town, but John and his sisters were gathered in her bedroom. As he read a solemn prayer, Susanna's demeanour was peaceful and calm. Before she lost her ability to speak, she asked her children to sing a psalm, which they did. They all mourned her loss deeply. She had brought them up to love the Lord and the Word of God. She was a good mother.

***

Methodism began to spread all over England. John and Charles Wesley, along with their many lay preachers, travelled the length and breadth of the nation, preaching and teaching the Bible. They set up new Methodist Societies. The men took every evangelistic opportunity that the Lord gave them to call men and women, boys, and girls to repent and follow Jesus.

'I look upon all the world as my parish,' said John in a letter to a friend. So he would not rest until he had pointed as many people that came across his path to the Saviour.

His brother Charles was particularly gifted in the way he was able to draw people into a new Methodist society. But John was especially gifted in leadership and organisational skills when it came to developing the new and existing societies.

Charles was a wonderful preacher, poet, and hymn-writer. He often composed hymns after significant events in his life.[6]

John had incredible energy and zeal, preaching over fifteen sermons most weeks, travelling by horse up to five thousand miles in an average year. When he got older, he travelled by chaise[7] across the land. He had a great knack for reading books quickly when he was travelling on horseback. This was not a talent most accomplished riders had. And yet John still managed to find time for his prolific writing of books, hymns, and letters.

Both Charles and John spent time writing in their journals, believing the exercise to be of great value to future generations who wanted to know how the Methodist work began. They would leave nothing out. They would not only record the good experiences in their life and work, but also the many bad experiences they encountered, especially in those early years of itinerant gospel ministry.

During a visit to the Midlands and north of England, the men experienced some fierce opposition to their work. In the town of Walsall, Charles stood on the steps of the market house and began to preach. A crowd gathered about him, and they began to roar and shout so that his message could not be heard. They constantly

---

6. See the *Fact File* called 'Hymns' in the back of the book.
7. A *chaise* is a small horse-drawn carriage that can accommodate one or two people.

threw stones at him, and many hit their target. But Charles kept on preaching. Calmly he implored them to be reconciled to God. They continued to hound him until he left quietly through the band of rage-filled rioters.

Moving on from there to Sheffield, Charles went to the place where the little society of Methodists met regularly. A large number of agitators had also gathered to cause trouble for him. The moment that Charles went to the pulpit to preach, the mob started to raise their voices in opposition to him. A naval officer swore loudly and began to oppose everything that Charles was saying. Charles just ignored him and carried on. Then came the stoning. To save the faithful Methodists from being hurt, Charles shouted loudly that he would preach outside. The mob followed him.

A naval officer with the rank of captain, grabbed Charles and started to verbally abuse him. With dignity and strength from the Lord, Charles kept on preaching the gospel to the mob. More stones were thrown at him, many striking him in the face. He did not stop. Charles preached on through the torment. When he had finished preaching, he prayed for his attackers. The captain was enraged and forced his way back through the crowd to get at Charles. He even drew his sword and pointed it at Charles' chest. Charles did not retract from the sharp and glistening edge, but rather pressed his chest further against the tip of the steel blade. He looked the captain straight in the eye and smiled. Then he calmly said, 'I fear God and honour the King.' The captain's angry expression fell from his face. He let out a deep sigh and sheathed his sword. Charles was a worthy opponent. Then the captain quietly left the place.

Charles and a few others went next door to the home of a local Methodist, Mr Bennet, to spend time in prayer. However, the rioters did not relent. They began to tear down the society-house while Charles and the others were praying and praising God. One of his group sent for the local police constable to come and put a stop to the wilful damage caused by the mob. Instead, the constable urged Charles to leave the town because his presence was the reason for all the disturbance.

'Thank you, Constable, for your advice,' said Charles. 'Please let me assure you that I shall not go a moment the sooner because of this uproar. I am sorry for your sakes that you do not have a magistrate here to enforce the law. As for me, I have my protection. I know my business, as I am sure that you know yours.'

The constable left and he encouraged the mob to press hard against Mr Bennet's door to break it open.

'I shall go out to them,' said Charles.

'You shall not,' retorted Mr Bennet. 'They are in vile humour. It would not be wise.'

'The Lord is my strength,' Charles affirmed.

'Well, ask him to strengthen that door too, so that it does not break,' said Mr Bennet.

The door did not break. The mob did not enter Mr Bennet's house that night. Instead, they attacked the society-house and pulled down one end of it.

The following day Charles went courageously into the centre of the town to preach. The noise of his opponents could be heard from a distance. Undeterred Charles began to preach the gospel. This time he was not opposed by those who had gathered to listen.

When his sermon was over, Charles walked through the open streets on his way back to Mr Bennet's house. There was a large crowd at his heels. He walked past the society-house and saw, to his astonishment, that there was not one stone left on top of another. Only the foundations remained.

Charles quickly nipped into Mr Bennet's house. The moment he was inside, the mob started to threaten to tear down the house. The windows were immediately smashed. Mr Bennet and his family were terrified. However, the mob did not enter the premises and dispersed that night, without harming anyone.

Early the next morning, Charles left the little Methodist society in Sheffield, rejoicing in God who had delivered them out of the mouth of the lions.

Riots and Opposition

John Wesley rode into the market town of Wednesbury in the West Midlands of England on 20 October, 1743. He made his way to the middle of the town then took out his Bible from his saddlebag. Turning to the letter of Hebrews he cleared his throat. Then he read chapter thirteen verse eight in a loud and distinct voice, 'Jesus Christ is the same yesterday, and today and for ever.'

A large crowd gathered around him to hear his message. John was surprised at the number. Nonetheless, he preached with all his might. No one heckled him or threw stones. The people listened carefully to the gospel of Jesus Christ being proclaimed by this small man with long wavy auburn locks. It was a peaceful meeting, for which John was grateful to God.

In the early part of the afternoon, John went to the home of Mr Francis Ward, who was the leader of the small local Methodist society in Wednesbury. John had hoped for a quiet afternoon at a writing desk. There were a few other members of the society there to spend time with their founder.

'Mr Wesley, come quick!' said Mr Ward as he looked through the window of the sitting room. John hastily joined Mr Ward at the window. There was a large angry mob heading straight for the house. Soon they were besieged by angry people swearing and shouting for Mr Wesley to be brought out to them.

'Gather everyone together, Mr Ward. We must pray,' said John. With everyone gathered in the sitting room they knelt to pray, begging God to disperse the angry mob. After half an hour of earnest prayer, miraculously the mob was gone.

'Now is the time for me to go,' said John.

'But the mob is gone, Mr Wesley. Won't you stay a while longer?' asked Mr Ward.

'It is always a pleasure to spend time in your company, Mr Wesley,' said one of the friends. 'Don't allow these people to deprive us of your company.'

Not wanting to offend anyone, John reluctantly agreed to stay a while longer and sat down. He felt uneasy. Deep down he knew what was coming to his hospitable and kind hosts.

By 5 p.m. that evening, the mob had returned, their numbers swelled by a group of people from the neighbouring mining town of Darlaston.

'Bring out the minister!' they cried. 'We will have the minister!'

The people in the house were quite afraid. The grand scale of opposition against the founder of Methodism was new to them, but sadly not to John. He bade one of them to go to the door and bring the gang leader into the house by the hand. He wanted to see if he could reason with him. Those in the room doubted he could.

One of them obliged and moments later returned with the leader of the mob. All could see the fury on the antagonist's face. John smiled and spoke to him gently. The ringleader's countenance changed. 'See, how the lion has become like a lamb,' thought John.

'Go and fetch one or two of your more angry companions,' said John to the gang leader. 'Bring them here to me.'

The man did as he was told. He brought two more people in before John. He spoke softly to them for a couple of minutes, and they became as calm as their leader.

Then John told them, 'Make a pathway into the crowd, and bring a chair with you.' They did as he instructed. When he was in the middle of the crowd, he took the chair and stood on it, so that he might speak to the people.

'What do you want with me?' asked John.

'We want you to go with us to the magistrate,' came the reply from the crowd.

'That I will, with all my heart,' replied John. He then began to speak of the love of God in Christ Jesus.

Someone in the crowd shouted out, 'This man is an honest gentleman, and we will spill our blood to defend him.'

'Shall we go to the magistrate tonight, or in the morning?' asked John.

Most of the mob cried, 'Tonight! Tonight!'

'Very well. Let us go,' declared John, jumping off the chair, and setting off briskly at the head of the crowd. Two or three hundred people followed him. The rest of the mob went back to their homes.

Four of the Wednesbury Methodist Society went with John on this journey that was fraught with peril. William Sitch held John by the arm. Joan Parks, Edward Slater, and John Griffiths walked close by. They had only walked a mile when darkness came upon them. Heavy rain poured down from the night sky. A couple of people were sent ahead to Bentley Hall, to the home of Mr Justice Lane who was the local magistrate.

When Mr Lane was informed that a crowd was bringing Mr Welsey before him he asked, 'What have I got to do with Mr Wesley? Go and carry him back again.'

When the mob arrived at the door, however, they started knocking loudly.

'We are here to speak with the magistrate,' said one of the mob, gruffly to the servant at the door.

'Mr Lane is in bed. Please go away,' came the firm but polite reply.

'Go and get him up,' demanded the gruff man.

Mr Lane's son moved to the open doorway, manoeuvring the servant gently aside. 'What is the matter?' he said impatiently.

Pointing to Mr Wesley, the gruff man said, 'Well, if it please you, they sing psalms all day. Not only that, they make folks rise at five in the morning. And what would your Worship advise us to do?'

'To go home,' advised young Mr Lane, 'and be quiet.' He closed the door, indicating that the conversation was over.

'What will we do now?' the gruff man asked the mob.

'Right. Let's go to Justice Persehouse at Walsall,' came the reply from someone in the middle of the pack.

'Aye!' shouted the mob in agreement. It was a further three miles east from Bentley Hall. Soaked and dejected, they began their march to Walsall. They arrived at their destination about seven in the evening only to discover that Mr Persehouse had gone to bed.

'What will we do now?' the gruff man asked the mob, again.

'I'm fed up. I'm going home,' came a reply from one of them.

'Me too. I'm soaked,' said another. 'What about Mr Wesley?'

'Some of us will take him home, I suppose,' said the gruff man.

The mob decided to head back to Wednesbury, with fifty of them agreeing to take John safely home. They had barely gone a hundred metres when a large Walsall gang ambushed them. A terrible fight broke out. The Wednesbury mob was wet and weary, and they were overwhelmed by the larger numbers and physical freshness of their enemies. Many of them were knocked to the ground. The rest ran away leaving poor John and his Methodist friends at the mercy of this new mob. The roaring shouts from the gang was such that John thought it impossible to speak and be heard. So, he said nothing.

The mob dragged John back into town. One man tried to strike John on the back of the head with a long stick made from oak, but every time he tried, the blow was turned aside from John. He saw a door of a house partially opened and made a dash for it. However, a man caught him by his long auburn hair and pulled him back into the middle of the crowd.

They marched him from one end of the town to the other. William Sitch was still holding John by the arm through it all. John was trying to make his voice heard above the din of the mob, but their angry shouts were too loud. Then he noticed the door of the candlemaker's shop open. John made his way to the door, but the proprietor was standing in his way, and would not allow him to enter.

'This lot will pull the shop down around my ears if I let you in here,' the shopkeeper said to John.

John turned to the mob. He shouted, 'Are you willing to hear me speak?'

'No, no! Knock his brains out! Kill him at once!' shouted some of the crowd.

'No, not yet. Let's hear him first,' said others.

For a moment, the noise of the angry crowd abated.

'What evil have I done? asked John. 'Which of you have I wronged in word or deed?' There was no response from the mob. John then spoke to them about the love of God for over fifteen minutes, until his voice gave way.

The clamour for John's blood began again, only this time with more ferocity. 'Take him away! Take him away!' they cried. The strength in his voice returned and John began to pray in a loud voice.

The leader of the mob was remarkably changed by what he heard and saw of John, and said to him, 'Sir, I will spend my life for you. Follow me, and not one soul here shall touch a hair of your head.' A few others agreed and got close to John, to protect him.

The shopkeeper, who was also the mayor of the town, cried out to the mob, 'This is shameful! Let him go!' At the same time, the town's butcher was pulling four or five people away, in full agreement to let John and his friends go.

The mob parted, and John's newly formed escort took him down the wet and slippery cobbles of the road to the flooded brook at the bottom of the town. When they reached the footbridge, however, the opposition rallied again. 'Throw him in!' shouted some of them. A man hit John hard in the mouth. His escort directed John down one side of the bridge, over the mill dam and through the meadows to safety.

William Sitch walked next to John as Edward Slater, John Griffiths and Joan Parks led the way in front. They were close to Wednesbury when John asked William a searching question.

'What did you expect, when the mob came upon us, William?'

'To die for Him who had died for us,' came William's noble reply.

'What about you, Joan? Were you afraid when they tore you away from me?'

Joan slowed her pace until she was next to John. 'I was no more afraid than I am now,' she said. 'I could trust God for you, as well as for myself. From the beginning, I had a full persuasion that God would deliver you. I knew not how. But I had left that to Him.'

When they reached Mr Ward's home at ten o'clock that night, the weary group found the occupants were praying for them. Their horrible tribulation had lasted five hours.

In those days, no matter where they went, John and Charles experienced terrible opposition. Riots often broke out, caused simply by their presence in towns and cities across England. But they did not want to confine their ministry and God's salvation to England. It was their great desire to bring the gospel of Christ to other parts of the British Isles, even across the Irish Sea.

Perhaps the Wesleys would be better received in Ireland.

Across the Irish Sea

The beautiful city of Dublin lies on the spectacular east coast of Ireland. Founded in A.D. 840 by the Vikings, over time it has been transformed into one of the most elegant cities in Europe. It was also to be the first port of call for the Methodist movement in Ireland.

Remarkably it wasn't John or Charles Wesley, but Thomas Williams who was the first Methodist preacher there.

Williams began his ministry in England and often helped John on his journeys throughout the country. It wasn't until the summer of 1747 that Williams crossed the Irish Sea to work in Dublin. He began to preach in Oxmantown Green in the city, as he did not have a building in which to meet. Still, he drew large crowds to hear the gospel of Christ. And the Lord made his open-air work successful, as many people became members of the first Methodist society in Ireland.

After a while, a house at the corner of Marlborough Street and Talbot street in Dublin was offered as a meeting place.

Mr Williams wrote to John Wesley, giving him a full account of his labours in the Lord. When John read of his success, he decided that he must visit.

On the Sunday morning, 9 August, 1747, John landed with his travelling companion, Mr Trembath, at St George's Quay, Dublin. Shortly after his arrival, John heard the bells of St Mary's Church ring out, calling people to the church service. He decided to go to the service before making his way to his lodgings. John was to stay with a Mr Lunnell, who collected him after the church service and took John and his friend to his house.

That afternoon, John penned a short note to the curate of St Mary's, offering his assistance while he was there. The offer was warmly received by the curate, and he invited John to preach that evening at St Mary's.

Early the following morning, John met the little Methodist society that had been started by Mr Williams, and encouraged them with the gospel. So many had gathered that there was not enough room for all of them. Then he made his way to visit the curate of St Mary's at his kind invitation. The curate spoke well of John's preaching, but confessed that he was not favourable towards lay preachers, or open-air preaching. He warned John that the Archbishop of Dublin would not permit any irregularities like these in his diocese. John listened respectfully to the curate's warning, but paid no attention to it, for he preferred to obey God rather than men. He was going to preach in the streets, on the highways, or wherever he could get people to hear the gospel of Jesus. And he was not going to stop his lay preachers doing the same.

Nonetheless, as a clergyman in the Church of England, John preferred to work in co-operation with those in ecclesiastical authority if he could, so he paid a visit to Dr Charles Cobbe, the Anglican Archbishop of Dublin. The meeting was cordial enough, but John failed to change Cobbe's mind about open-air ministry or Methodism. Throughout the land, every pulpit would be closed to the Methodists.

Undeterred by the cold welcome from his Anglican colleagues, John preached morning and evening to large congregations at the house. Many stood outside just to hear him. He found it interesting that most of the people he met were not Irish at all, but had moved to Ireland from England.

He noticed that the native Irish did not want to deviate from the Catholic religion of their forefathers. This made John critical of the Protestants' ineffective evangelism in Ireland.

'Is it any wonder, that those who are born Roman Catholic generally live and die that way, when the Protestants can find no better way to convert them than Penal Laws and Acts of Parliament.'[1]

For now, all those he met were cordial and ready to hear his message with gladness. Those who professed membership of the Methodist society in Dublin were

---

1. John Wesley's *Journal*, Volume 2, page 68, entry for Saturday, 15 August, 1747.

found to be strong in faith, which greatly pleased John. He returned to England at the end of the month, content that the society in Ireland was thriving by the grace of God.

As usual it was not long before opposition broke out against the Methodists. Dublin had a lawless reputation, with robberies and murders being frequently committed in the streets. The butchers of Ormond market and the Liberty weavers from the centre of Dublin would sometimes meet and fight until one or more were deceased. On one occasion a constable was beaten to death in the open streets and hung up on a lamppost as a sign of victory for the oppressed. No one was called to account for it. It's no wonder therefore that the Methodists were roughly treated on every side.

Roman Catholic and Protestant mobs abused them. One Sunday evening, about a week before Charles travelled to Dublin, they surrounded the house where the society met. As members went out to the mob, some were knocked down and beaten, while the others retreated back into the room. The mob broke down the door, tore down the desk and other fittings and furnishings before dragging them out into the street, and burning them.

The authorities could do little to help. The Lord Mayor granted warrants to arrest the rioters. A few were sent to prison to await trial, but when the time came, the jury threw out all the charges, abandoning the Methodists to the fury of their opponents. Yet the Methodists remained steadfast in their faith during these trials, resolved to die rather than deny their Lord.

It was during these circumstances that Charles arrived in Dublin, on 9 September, 1747. He was accompanied by Mr Perronet, the son of a Kentish clergyman. They went on their way to the ruined meeting house in Marlborough Street. An angry and insolent mob followed them, hurling insults at them as they walked to the meeting house.

When they arrived, they found a few Methodist people were there to greet them. These brave souls were defiant of the mob; unafraid of the threat the mob posed to their wellbeing, and expectant of a good message from Mr Wesley. He preached unmolested.

A fortnight later Charles made his way to Oxmantown Green, to preach the cross of Christ to the Roman Catholic and Protestant crowd that gathered to hear him. No one shouted at him, or threw stones. Instead, they listened attentively to the gospel. Charles noticed that many of his hearers were crying when they heard about God's love for them.

The peace of that event, however, was overturned by continuous bouts of opposition throughout the rest of his visit. And as it was not feasible to continue to meet in the ruins of the house in Marlborough Street, Charles purchased a house in Dolphin's Barn in Cork Street. He turned the whole downstairs room into a preaching room, with two rows of benches and a pulpit at the end. The rooms above were suitable accommodation for visiting preachers, like his brother John.

At the beginning of his ministry in Ireland Charles was often opposed by violent mobs. By the time Charles had been in Dublin for two months, however, he found the people were generally more welcoming. Even the mayor of Dublin declared that he would imprison anyone who verbally abused the Methodists on the street!

When another three months had passed, Charles felt that the Methodist cause was established well enough for him to leave it for a while and go further inland. Fifty miles from Dublin, in a place called Tyrrellspass in County Westmeath, Charles preached on the 'Parable of the Two Sons.'[2]

He was overjoyed to see how the people devoured every word of his message. He made a comment about them in his journal.

> 'God has begun a great work here. The people of Tyril's-pass were wicked to a proverb; swearers, drunkards, Sabbath-breakers, thieves etc from time immemorial. But now the scene is entirely changed. Not an oath is heard, or a drunkard seen among them. They are turned from darkness to light. Near one hundred are joined in Society, and following hard after the pardoning of God.'[3]

Moving on to Athlone, a town on the border between County Westmeath and County Roscommon, things were different. As Charles and his companions were

---

2. Matthew 21:28-32.

3. Charles Wesley's *Journal*, Volume 2, page 2, entry for Monday, 8 February, 1748.

riding up a little hill, some Roman Catholic men began to throw stones at them. One of the horsemen, Mr Healey, was knocked off his horse and lay motionless on the ground. Charles could see that more thugs were beginning to gather. The ruffian who had knocked Mr Healey to the ground then struck the defenceless servant of God on the face with his wooden club.

'Stop it!' Charles cried out. The villain turned to strike Charles instead. Charles was sure that one more blow to his friend's head would have killed him. The ruffians had gathered enough stones of varying sizes to cause serious damage to the small group of Methodists. The horses neighed and reared as stones intended for their riders struck them too. A large stone hit another of Charles' friends on the head and disabled him for a moment. Another missile hit Charles on the back and winded him.

They tried to retreat a short distance but were reluctant to leave the incapacitated Mr Healey at the hands of his attackers. They rode back to the field of battle only to find that most of the mob were gone. However, the man who wounded Mr Healey had stayed to finish the job with his knife, swearing that he would cut him up.

A poor woman appeared from her hut nearby and came to Mr Healey's assistance, telling the attacker in no uncertain terms not to harm the injured Mr Healey anymore. The man's lip curled in anger. He lifted Mr Healey's whip and struck the woman hard with it, but she would not relent. Eventually she managed to get Mr Healey away from his attacker and with the help of her husband carried him to safety into their home.

Charles and the others found Mr Healey bleeding badly in the woman's hut and bundled him onto his horse. They then headed for Athlone as quickly as they could. The local doctor cleaned his wounds and bandaged him up. When the locals heard what had happened, they were outraged at the actions of the mob. Charles was grateful that none of his party had lost their lives.

On another occasion in the north of Ireland, Charles was preaching in the fields in the parish of Killyleagh in County Down. A large group of people who did not approve of his teaching gathered to do him harm. Charles made his escape along the Shore Road heading to a little village that overlooked Strangford Lough called Killinchy. He could hear the mob gaining on him. Coming to 'Islandbawn Farm' in the townland of Ringhaddy on the lough shore, Charles sought refuge from the farmer's wife, Mrs Moore.

'Forgive this intrusion, madam,' panted Charles when the farmhouse door opened. 'My name is Reverend Charles Wesley, at your service. I was hoping that I may find refuge here for a moment ...'

'Refuge? Who from?' asked Mrs Moore surprised.

'I appear to have a large unsavoury mob in pursuit of me,' replied Charles. 'I fear they do not like my message of God's love.'

Taking pity on him she commanded, 'Quick then, come with me.' Mrs Moore led Charles down to the Milk House at the bottom of the garden. 'Hide in there,' she told him. Charles entered and crouched down behind some tall milk churns near the back wall.

Soon the mob came and stopped at the farm. The gang leader banged on the farmhouse door. He was quickly greeted by a disapproving look from Mrs Moore who did not like the abuse he was giving her door.

'And what can I do for you?' she scowled.

'Mrs Moore, we are in pursuit of a terrible fella, so we are,' said the man. A roar of agreement went up from the mob.

'What is so terrible about this fella you are chasin'?' she asked.

'Oh he's a real ruffian, so he is, Mrs Moore, sayin' all sorts of terrible things about our church, so he does.'

'Terrible things, eh,' repeated Mrs Moore. 'Like what?'

'Like … like … well that doesn't matter, have you seen him?'

'It doesn't matter?' said Mrs Moore incredulously. She looked around at the mob, then looked the leader straight in the eye. 'Just look at you there, with all these people behind you. I've known you since you were a wee lad. You think you're a big man, but yer wee coat still fits you!'

The mob roared with laughter.

'Now Mrs Moore, that's enough of that!' the man shouted over the din of the mob. 'Your farm is a perfect spot to hide, so it is. Sure, you don't mind if we have a wee look about,' said the mob leader, as some of his party broke off to scour the farmyard.

'You're all looking a bit thirsty there,' said Mrs Moore quickly. 'Can I offer youse some milk? I have plenty in the Milk House.'

'Well, that would be grand, Mrs Moore,' replied the man.

'Just wait here and I'll fetch some,' said Mrs Moore. She scurred off down to the Milk House at the bottom of the garden.

'Mr Wesley,' she whispered. Charles poked his head above the milk churns. 'Get yerself through that window and hide under some bushes near the stream that runs to the back there,' she commanded. 'I can't hold them off you for long.' She grabbed a bucket and filled it with milk from one of the milk churns. She left by the door as Charles scrambled through the back window. He found a good hiding place under some bushes by the stream and did not move a muscle. He could hear the noise of his hunters all around him.

Like so many of his hymns that were written in times of trial and opposition, Charles began to think of words to another hymn of praise as he lay under the bushes. He would call it, 'Jesu, lover of my soul.'

After a while, the voices of his pursuers faded and then they were gone. Charles headed for Killinchy, unharmed.

The Irish mobs often gave Charles and John a heated reception when they visited their country. Over the years, the Wesleys made countless trips to the island to preach the gospel of Christ.

During a visit to Cork in 1750, the mayor of the town sent the town drummers and his sergeants to disturb the congregation that had gathered to hear John preach. They came down to the preaching place accompanied by a large and unruly mob. The drummers were noisy, but John preached on. Then he went out to ask one of the sergeants to keep the peace.

'Sir, I have no orders to do that!' came the reply.

The mob threw whatever came to hand at John, but nothing made an impact. He walked forward quietly and looked at each person as he moved. The mob opened up as he passed along. When he reached his friend's house, a Roman Catholic woman stood at the entranceway to block his passage. Just then, one of the mob swung a fist at John, which missed him but knocked the woman down to the ground. John looked at her on the ground. Then he stepped over her and into the house. No one followed him.

***

It was not all doom and gloom for the Wesleys. Over the years of courageous gospel ministry in Ireland, thousands of people were brought from darkness to light; from serving the devil to serve the true and living God of the Bible.

Only five years after the work in Ireland began, in the summer of 1752, the first Methodist Conference of members was held in Limerick, a city in the west of Ireland.

In 1787, at Chrome Hill in the parish of Lambeg near Lisburn, John entwined two beech saplings as a symbol of his hope for a growing relationship between the Church of Ireland and the Methodists.[4]

John visited Ireland for the last time in 1789, at the age of eighty-six years old. It was a successful tour of the country, teaching the Bible and encouraging the Irish Methodists to keep on following Christ. He was treated like royalty wherever he went – quite a different reception to the violence of those early days in Ireland.

On that last visit, when it was time to return home, a great crowd followed John down to the ship bound for England. Before he boarded, he called out a hymn which they all sang together. He kneeled and prayed for all those who were present and for God's blessing upon the Church, especially in Ireland. He then stood and shook hands with his well-wishers. Many wept. It was a most tender moment for John.

On board the vessel he looked at the multitude on the dock. He lifted his hands and blessed them in the name of Christ. Those looking upon his frail countenance waved their handkerchiefs goodbye until the ship was out of sight.

John never returned to Ireland.

---

4. Chrome Hill became the setting for the signing of the historic 'Church of Ireland – Methodist Covenant'. This happened in September 2002. The Covenant was signed by the President of the Methodist Church in Ireland, and the Church of Ireland Primate.

Love and Marriage

The large country mansion of Garth in Brecknockshire, South Wales, was the home of Marmaduke Gwynne; a powerful man in the county. He had a big family of nine children, and twenty servants and a domestic chaplain at his beck and call.

Charles first met Mr Gwynne in Bristol in 1745. Two years later, when he was visiting a clergyman whose church was not far from Garth, he met Miss Sarah Gwynne, or 'Sally' as she was known to family and friends. On that day Mr Gwynne had called at the clergyman's house to visit Charles and brought Sally with him. Charles was invited to preach at Garth and his message were received warmly by the family.

When Charles met Sally it was love at first sight but he was on his way to Ireland and his mission would last six months. On his return, in 1748, he detoured to Garth where the rain was lashing down, drenching Charles throughout.

Worn out and thoroughly soaked to the skin, Charles collapsed at Garth and spent ten days recovering from sickness. It wasn't all bad, as he was in the pleasant company of the Gwynne family, and of Sally in particular. He liked her very much. Fortunately for Charles, she liked him too.

Around the same time that Charles' affections were growing for Sally, his brother John was returning from another trip to Ireland, just in time to open the extension to the Kingswood school that he founded nine years before, in 1739, when it was built for the collier's children at Kingswood. John hoped to make it a thoroughly Christian school, for the benefit of Methodism in general. Who knew how many of the children would be preachers of the gospel in the future? The success of the school over the years now justified a larger school building.

John wrote the textbooks and worked hard to make the school successful, but his rules were severe. The children were required to get up at four in the morning. They were expected to spend time in prayer before attending a service which started at 5 a.m. Breakfast was at six, and lessons began at seven. They had to work for four hours. From eleven to twelve they engaged either in working or walking. Then lunch was served at noon. They started lessons again, after working in the garden or singing, from 1 p.m. until 5 p.m. in the afternoon. More private devotions followed. And then from six until seven that evening the children were expected to work, or walk, or pray some more. Supper came after that. Bed was at 8 p.m.

The children were constantly supervised. There were no holidays, or games.

Undoubtedly the rules were broken by everyone in the school. All fell short of John's high expectations. As he got older, he became disappointed with the school's performance, especially when pupil numbers dropped considerably over the years.

When the grand opening of the school extension was complete, John was back on the road for Newcastle. However, when he got there, he became ill with such a severe headache it made him feel physically sick. So, he went straight to bed to recover. It was most unlike John to stop working, so he must have been very ill indeed. He stayed at the Orphan House and was cared for by the housekeeper, Mrs Grace Murray.

Grace was widowed in 1742 when her husband, a sailor, was drowned at sea. She was now the trusted housekeeper of the Orphan House, and was at the forefront of the Christian work in that place. She also acted as the nurse to all the Methodist preachers in the area. At one time she had seven sick itinerants to care for, including Mr Bennet, whom she nursed for six months and was very fond of.

Affections grew between Grace and John during his recuperation at the Orphan House. Ten days later, when he was fully recovered, it was time for John to leave Newcastle. He expressed his conviction that God intended her to be his wife and hoped than when they met again, he would not have to leave her anymore.

Grace did not want them to part company and begged John to take her with him. So, John took Grace with him on his journey through the northern counties of Yorkshire and Derbyshire in England. Grace was a helpful accomplice to John and also to the Societies whom she met in those places.

They arrived in the Derbyshire town of Chinley and met Mr Bennet who was ministering to the Methodists in the area. Together the three travelled on to Astbury in Cheshire, where John left Grace in Bennet's care while he went on a preaching tour throughout Derbyshire. John was unaware that Bennet wanted to marry Grace too! Her affections fluctuated between John Wesley and John Bennet. She was not sure whom to marry. O the dilemma!

Meanwhile Charles was hoping to marry Sally Gwynne. There was a local minister from a church near Garth who also desired Sally Gwynne to be his bride! Charles knew that Mrs Gwynne would rather see her daughter Sally marry him than any other man in England, so he was not worried about the situation.

Charles contacted his brother John to gain his approval. He rarely did anything without getting his brother's opinion about it.

Sally Gwynne married Charles Wesley on 8th April 1749. His brother John conducted the ceremony. It was a grand occasion filled with joy and laughter. Grace accompanied John to the wedding.

The following week, Grace and John travelled to Ireland. They were together for three months ministering to the people of Ireland. John travelled about the country preaching and teaching the Bible. Grace visited the sick and prayed with those who sought God's forgiveness for their sins.

John's esteem for Grace increased each day they were together. Her devotion to the Lord and his work greatly impressed him. He wondered if she would make a good partner in life as well as in ministry. When they arrived in Dublin, they promised to marry each other. But it was not an official engagement.

Returning to England, they travelled from Bristol to London and then on to Newcastle. Doubts about marriage were looming in both their minds. But in Newcastle Grace affirmed her love for John. It was her desire that they should marry immediately. John wanted to get his brother Charles' approval, and inform the Methodist Societies of his intention to marry.

John wrote to Charles, who had moved to Bristol with Sally. When Charles read of John's intention to marry Grace, he was filled with dread. Charles believed that Grace, a mere household servant, was not worthy to marry his esteemed brother John, the founder of Methodism. He also thought the marriage would cause difficulties for Methodism in general, believing that their preachers would leave them if John insisted on marrying a housekeeper, for that was effectively her position at the Orphan House.

Charles hurried north on horseback to speak with John. He wanted to convince him that the marriage was not a good idea. He caught up with John at Whitehaven on the west coast of England. Try as he might, Charles could not convince him to change his mind about marrying Grace. It was clear that John wanted to marry Grace because of her good Christian character, and not because of what she did for work.

So, Charles changed tack. He decided he would try to convince Grace not to marry John instead. He sped south to the town of Hindley where Grace was staying. He managed to persuade Grace not to marry his brother. Then together they rode to Newcastle where Bennet had arrived from Derbyshire. Within a week, Grace and Bennet were married in Newcastle!

Charles had succeeded in his quest to save his brother from a terrible marriage, or so he thought. However, John would not learn of the marriage from his brother's lips.

George Whitefield invited John to Leeds, where he broke the painful news of the marriage between Grace and Bennet to him. The next day, Charles arrived in Leeds with Bennet and Grace. They wanted to see John.

It was a tense meeting at first. But it ended with a superficial reconciliation between them all.

The relationship between Charles and John, however, would never be the same again. Though his heart was heavy, John continued with his work, spending four months in Ireland, one month in Cornwall, as well as travelling to other parts of England for shorter visits.

John also travelled to Scotland for the first time in April 1751. Some Methodist Societies had been started in Dundee and John was urged to visit. He preached the gospel to a large attentive congregation in the East Lothian town of Musselburgh. Afterwards they urged him to stay, but his preaching itinerary would not permit it. However, John paid many visits to Scotland in his lifetime, encouraging the faithful to stick with Jesus.

In January 1751 John was called to Oxford to attend to some business at Lincoln College before travelling on to London for a short visit of preaching engagements. He planned another trip up north, but tragedy struck that prevented his movements in that direction.

As he was crossing London Bridge on foot, John slipped on some ice and twisted his ankle. He hobbled to two of his preaching engagements that day, but the pain was so great that he needed to rest. He therefore did not preach at the Foundery which was his third engagement that day. The journey north was no longer a possibility. Instead he moved into a room at the home of Mrs Mary Vazeille in Threadneedle Street.

Mary Vazeille, or 'Molly' as she was known to her friends, was a wealthy widow with four children. Charles and Sally Wesley knew her, having spent some time with Molly in her home the previous year. They liked her but thought she could be melancholic at times.

Molly took good care of John while he stayed with her. It didn't take long to nurse his injured ankle back to health. A romance blossomed quickly with John deciding that he would marry Molly. He informed Charles of his intention but did not reveal his bride's name to him. Charles had to find out from a friend that John was marrying Molly.

Naturally Charles did not approve. He did not feel that Molly possessed the spiritual qualities that would win the approval of the Methodists. John did not care what Charles thought about his marriage. As Charles prevented him from marrying Grace, the woman he loved, John was not going to allow Charles to interfere on this occasion.

Barely a week after arriving in Threadneedle Street, John and Molly were married at Wandsworth Parish Church in London. A fortnight later, John set out for Bristol, and Molly stayed in London. They had both agreed before the wedding that John should maintain his itinerant ministry at the usual pace. Just because he was married did not mean that he should slacken his preaching ministry.

The first four years of their marriage saw Molly travel extensively with John the length and breadth of the British Isles. By now there were very few instances of persecution for the Methodists, although a violent mob incident in Hull, in the north of England, disturbed Molly greatly.

It was gradually becoming clear that Molly was not cut out for the constant travel, lack of comfort and sheer weariness of the mission which John gladly endured. She had a bad temper, and became jealous of John's friendships with members of the Methodist Societies. This put their marriage under constant strain. It was not helped by John's voracious appetite for work.

John was constantly travelling and preaching. In addition, he was busily engaged in writing his 'Christian Library' as he called it; fifty volumes of religious writings from the early Church Fathers onwards. He even produced a dictionary with a witty title; 'The Complete English Dictionary, Explaining most of those Hard words which are found in the Best English Writers. By a Lover of Good English and Common Sense. N.B. – The Author assures you he thinks this is the best English Dictionary in the World!'

John became so sick during one of his preaching tours he had to retreat to the home of a friend in London for five weeks. He suffered from tuberculosis, an infectious disease that attacks the lungs. John thought he was going to die. The outlook was so grim John had already written the words for his gravestone. It read:

> Here lies
> The body of John Wesley
> A Brand, not once only, plucked out of the fire.
> He died of a consumption in the fifty-first year of his age,
> Leaving, after his debts were paid,
> not ten pounds behind him:
> Praying
> 'God be merciful to me an unprofitable servant!'[1]

John's prayer was for Molly and Charles to forget all the bad things that had happened between them in the

---

1. John Wesley's *Journal*, Volume 2, page 309, entry for Monday, 26 November, 1753.

past. Charles who had rushed to pray by his brother's bedside took hold of John's hand and agreed.

In answer to the prayers of family and friends, the Lord restored John to health slowly. It took nearly a year for John to recover fully from his illness. During his convalescence, he spent his time writing his 'Notes on the New Testament'. In his journal on Friday, 4 January, 1754, John confessed that it was

> *'a work which I should scarce ever have attempted, had I not been so ill as not to be able to travel or preach, and yet so well as to be able to read or write.'*

While he convalesced, the leadership of the Methodist movement fell on Charles' shoulders. He didn't like being in charge. He made it absolutely clear that should anything happen to John to keep him from leading the Methodist movement permanently, Charles was not going to be his successor. He had stepped back from the itinerant ministry when he got married and started a family. Charles' work was now confined mostly to Bristol, where he lived, and London.

Once John was fully recovered, he got back on his horse to travel the highways and byways of the nation. There was still much work for the Lord to be done.

A Time of Grief

By 1757 riots and mob violence against the Wesleys had almost stopped. The years that followed witnessed many Methodist Societies spring up all over the country. The Methodist movement was well organised, thanks to John's great ability to carefully administrate it. A small army of Methodist itinerant preachers were working hard for the Lord all over the United Kingdom.

Methodism spread through America by leaps and bounds. George Whitefield had been extremely busy, preaching and teaching tirelessly along the east coast, from Boston in the north, to Savannah in the south. His voracious appetite for work was similar to John's. When George was begged by those who loved him to take more care of himself, he would often say, 'It is better to wear out rather than rust out.' Through sickness and health George laboured, refusing to stop.

George wrote a letter to Charles during the summer of 1754 from the Carolinas in America.

'My health is wonderfully preserved. My vomiting has stopped, and though I ride whole nights, and have been frequently exposed to great thunders, violent lightnings and heavy rains, yet I am rather better than usual, and as far as I can judge am not yet to die. O that I might at length begin to live. I am ashamed of my sloth and lukewarmness, and long to be on the stretch for God.'[1]

It was in Savannah, where John had ministered many years before, that George set up an orphanage called 'Bethesda' which means 'House of Mercy'. Any time that George was back in England, he would always raise funds for 'Bethesda'.

After a meeting with George in February 1769, John wrote in his journal, 'I had one more agreeable conversation with my old friend and fellow labourer George Whitefield. His soul appeared to be vigorous still, but his body was sinking rapidly.'[2]

It was only a matter of time before George did in fact 'wear out'. After spending four years in England preaching the gospel and raising money for 'Bethesda', George returned to America in September 1769.

On his arrival George was received with public honours by the Governor and council of the Savannah colony. The orphanage was in a good financial position. Two new wings had been built and other buildings were being pushed forward for completion.

His friends, however, were grieved to see how much George had aged while he was away. He suffered from asthma and chest pains caused by a low blood flow to the heart called angina. He also had a rare unknown

1. *George Whitefield and the Great Awakening* by John Pollock, London, 1972, page 246.
2. John Wesley's *Journal*, Volume 3, page 354, entry for Monday, 27 March, 1769.

condition which caused his face to puff up and turn red. Not surprisingly these things made him irritable at times.

When he set about another preaching tour his health appeared to be good. Enthusiastic crowds gathered to hear the gospel wherever he went.

On 29 September, George rode wearily into the town of Exeter, in New Hampshire. He planned to dine at a friend's house, and then travel on to Newbury Port, where he had agreed to preach the next day.

News of his arrival excited the locals. The ministers of the town begged George for a sermon. He agreed.

When the time came for him to preach, one of the ministers looked at George and exclaimed, 'Sir, you are more fit to go to bed than to preach!'

'That is true, sir,' George confirmed. He clasped his hands together and looked up to heaven and prayed, 'Lord Jesus, I am weary in your work, but I am not weary of your work. If I have not finished my course[3] let me go and speak for you once more in the fields, and seal your truth, and come home and die!'

With heightened anticipation the entire district of men, women, boys, and girls descended upon the field that Saturday afternoon, to hear George preach. His voice was strong as he proclaimed the glories of Christ for two hours. Then he left the town for Newbury Port, as the guest of the local minister there.

At supper with his hosts, George did not eat, drink, or talk that much. He retired to bed before the end of

---

3. 2 Timothy 4:7.

the meal. At two in the morning, he woke unable to catch his breath, thinking it was an asthma attack brought on by exhaustion. He died during the early hours of 30 September, 1770. He was only fifty-five years old.

News of his death reached John and Charles soon after. The brothers were greatly saddened to learn of the death of their friend. Of course, they had their disagreements with George Whitefield in the past, especially concerning the Bible's teaching about election[4], that God calls some to eternal life, but not all are saved. Yet any breach of friendship was soon mended, witnessed by the fact that George would often preach in the Wesleyan chapels when he returned from America to England. The three men never allowed their differences to destroy the mutual affection and regard they felt for one another.

John was once asked mischievously by a Methodist lady, if he believed he would meet George Whitefield in heaven. He thought about it for a moment. 'No, Madam,' John concluded. 'George Whitefield, will be so near the "Throne of Grace", that a sinner such as I am will never get a glimpse of him.'

It had long been agreed between George and John that the survivor should preach the sermon at his friend's funeral. On 18 November, 1770, a service was held in the Tottenham Court Road Tabernacle[5] in

---

4. For more information on the disagreement about *Election*, turn to the Fact File called 'Controversies' at the back of the book.

5. A *Tabernacle* is a building named after the 'Tent of Meeting', that is, the meeting-place of God and his people in the wilderness (Exodus 33:7-11).

London, and later that afternoon at the Tabernacle near Moorfields, where George Whitefield had ministered during his life in England.

Each building was full of people who had travelled from all over the country. The Lord gave strength to John's voice, enabling him to be heard by those who stood by the doorways. He spoke God's Word to them, seeking to comfort those who were feeling convicted of their own sin and mortality during the sad occasion. He pointed them to Jesus, the One who has the power to forgive sin and give the gift of eternal life. John also wanted to challenge those who were too comfortable in this life, and had no time for Christ, imploring all of them to place their trust in him and know the fullness of his love.

It was a sad occasion for John, to remember his friend before those large congregations. He took the time to record his feelings as he mourned the loss of a dear brother in the Lord.

> 'It was an awful season. All were as still as night. Most appeared to be deeply affected, and an impression was made on many, which, I hope, will not be quickly erased[6] ... In every place, I wish to show all possible respect to the memory of that great and good man.'[7]

The following year, 1771, Charles moved with his family to Chesterfield Street in Marylebone, in London.

---

6. John Wesley's *Journal*, Volume 3, page 421, entry for Saturday, 10 November, 1770.

7. John Wesley's *Journal*, Volume 3, page 422, entry for Wednesday, 2 January, 1771.

Over the years he and Sally had eight children, five of whom sadly died. Only Charles junior, Sarah and Samuel survived.

All three children were musical. Sarah could sing and play the harpsichord. Both Charles junior and Samuel were gifted organists and composers. Charles junior even gave regular recitals before King George III.

The family loved to host musical evenings which were attended by many of the leading members of society. General Oglethorpe, the Governor of Georgia, now more than eighty years old, made an appearance at one of the soirees on 25 February, 1781. When General Oglethorpe saw John there, he kissed his hand as a token of respect.

Charles' immense love of writing hymns and poetry continued. It was how he expressed his new life in Christ. He inherited this gift from his father, Samuel Wesley. Charles was free to express the unspeakable joy he felt in the Lord. Hymn after hymn flowed from his pen. He wrote and published thousands of hymns and poems. But now that he was back in London, he was also in a good position to help John, by relieving him of some of the demands made upon his brother's time. Charles visited the jails in London frequently, having the same concern for the inmates that he had shown when he was a younger man. He also preached at the City Road Chapel, which was opened by John in 1778 to replace the Foundery. The Foundery chapel had served them so well in the early years of the Methodist movement in London but had run into disrepair.

Home life was not as good for John as it was for Charles. Molly's unpredictable moods often dictated the atmosphere in the home. Unfortunately, she was in a foul temper most of the time when John was around the house. She was verbally and physically aggressive with him. However, John never lost his composure when the interactions with his wife were fraught with tension. It was no surprise that Molly left John in 1775, vowing never to return.

She died in Camberwell in south London in 1781, when John was away preaching in the west of England.

When he returned to London in October that year, he was told of her death.

> 'I came to London, and was informed that my wife died on Monday. This evening she was buried, though I was not informed of it till a day or two after.'[8]

It was a sad end to a difficult relationship in John's life.

***

In 1775, war broke out in America between the British and the colonists of thirteen British ruled colonies. It was called, 'The War of Independence.' The war had drastically weakened the Church of England's presence in America, making it nearly impossible for the thousands of Methodists there to receive the Lord's Supper or baptism.

John received an impassioned plea from Francis Asbury, the Methodist leader in America, asking him

---

8. John Wesley's *Journal*, Volume 4, page 218, entry for Friday, 12 October, 1781.

to ordain Methodist lay preachers to provide this vital ministry. The request was problematic. If John agreed to the request, it would undoubtedly lead to a permanent split from the Church of England.

Charles and John had always been against the Methodist movement breaking away from the Church of England, Charles especially so. From the beginning, the Methodist movement had some members who tried to encourage John to lead them away. It was a good job that Charles worked hard to keep the unity between Methodism and the Church of England. He felt strongly that Methodism should be kept within the Church of England.

John's personal convictions about how the Church of England was organised and governed changed over the years. He believed that bishops[9] and presbyters[10] were effectively one and the same office in the church. If this was true, as John believed it to be, he felt that he possessed as much authority to ordain men to ministry as any bishop in the Church of England did.

Although he believed he had the right to ordain others, John didn't fulfil Mr Asbury's request, because Charles was completely against it. Instead, John went to Dr Lowth, the Bishop of London, to see if he could help. Sadly, the bishop felt that he could not, due to the Americans' status as 'rebellious subjects' of the Crown.

---

9. In the Church of England, a **bishop** has the oversight of churches within his area, known as a Diocese.

10. A **presbyter** is the term given to a minister who has the oversight of a local church.

Mr Asbury wanted to see John back in America, but that was not going to happen. John was fully committed to the Lord's work at home. Instead, John ordained Dr Thomas Coke as the 'Superintendent' to oversee the work in America. Mr Asbury was to be his colleague, possessing the same authority as Dr Coke over the Methodist ministry in America. And with John's blessing, both Dr Coke and Mr Asbury could ordain men with the power to administer the sacraments of the Lord's Supper and baptism in America.

It was a huge step towards Methodism leaving the Church of England. But it didn't end there. After careful thought, John did the same thing the following year, and ordained three lay preachers to administer the Sacraments in Scotland. It was inevitable that John would eventually ordain men for ministry in England.

Charles was greatly disturbed by his brother's actions, but there was nothing he could do about it.

John decided to publish a statement justifying his action, but Charles couldn't get his head around it. He admitted to a friend in a letter that he could,

> 'Scarcely yet believe it, that in his eighty-second year my brother, my old intimate friend and companion, should have assumed the character of a bishop, ordained elders, consecrated a bishop (Dr Coke), and sent him to ordain the lay preachers in America! I was then in Bristol, at his elbow, but he never gave me the least hint of his intention.'[11]

---

11. Letter to Dr Chandler on 28 April, 1785.

Even at this stage, John confirmed to his brother that he was still a member of the Church of England and declared that he would not leave it. Charles wanted to believe him, but John's actions made it difficult. Only time would tell.

Give God the Glory

What would happen to Methodism when John and Charles were no longer able to lead it? This was the important question that was put to the Methodist Conference in Bristol during 1784. Before the matter was settled, however, John became dreadfully sick. No one expected him to get better.

A trusted friend was by his bedside. John shared some personal thoughts with him. 'I have been reflecting on my past life,' he whispered.

'Oh yes?' came the quizzical reply from his friend.

'I have been wandering up and down the country between fifty and sixty years, endeavouring in my poor way to do a little good to my fellow-creatures,' continued John weakly. 'And now it is probable that there are but a few steps between me and death.'

The sorrowful look on his friend's face spoke of the anguish many like him would experience at John's death. Not noticing, John went on. 'What have I to trust to for salvation? I can see nothing that I have done or suffered that will bear looking at. I have no other plea than this: I the chief of sinners am. But Jesus died for me.'

For eighteen days his friend nursed John back from the brink of death and into the land of the living. He recovered well. But his absence from the Methodist cause during that time highlighted the need to put a successor in place.

A 'Deed of Declaration' was written by John.[1] The deed declared that after his death, the authority to appoint preachers would fall to Charles. When Charles died, then it would pass to the body of the annual Methodist Conference.

As the month of January 1788 advanced, Charles became physically weak. He wasn't ill with a fever; neither was he in any pain. He was just old, and felt worn out.

Confined to bed, Charles' devoted wife, Sally often sat by his bed to read the Bible to him. One day, late in the month of March, she turned to the words that the apostle Paul wrote to the church at Corinth. Clearly and softly, she read, 'So we do not lose heart. Though our outer self is wasting away, our inner self is being renewed day by day. For this light momentary affliction is preparing for us an eternal weight of glory beyond all comparison, as we look not to the things that are seen but to the things that are unseen. For the things that

---

1. The ***Deed of Declaration*** also contained the names of one hundred preachers chosen by John Wesley, who were to form the Methodist Conference.

are seen are transient, but the things that are unseen are eternal.'[2]

'Amen,' replied Charles peacefully. A moment of silence passed between them. Then Charles made a request.

'Sally, I am too weak to lift my pen. Would you write down some words for me?'

'Of course, my love,' replied Sally. She found some paper, a quill and ink on his writing desk by the window. 'I'm ready.'

Charles took a breath, and began to dictate his last poem.

> 'In age and feebleness extreme
> Who shall a sinful worm redeem?
> Jesus, my only hope thou art,
> Strength of my failing flesh and heart;
> Oh, could I catch a smile from thee,
> And drop into eternity!'

'Charles, that is beautiful.'

'Thank you, my dear.' He closed his eyes. It was time to rest.

For much of his remaining time left on earth, Charles was unconscious. His life was near its end.

On Saturday, 29 March, 1788, his family entered his room and stood around his bed. His daughter Sarah took his frail hand and sat by his side. The only sounds were the gentle last breaths of Charles Wesley, the great preacher, hymnwriter and poet.

And then all was quiet.

---

2. 2 Corinthians 4:16-18

John was in Staffordshire in the West Midlands of England at the time of his brother's passing.

There was a mistake made in the address of the letter informing John of Charles' death which meant he didn't find out about it until the day before the funeral. He was too far away in the north of England to join the mourners in the graveyard of the old parish church at Marylebone, in London, where Charles was buried.

John wanted Charles to be buried in the grounds of the City Road Chapel. He was quite annoyed that Charles did not want to be buried there. In a final gesture of Charles' dislike of the idea of separation from the Church of England, he wanted to be buried in a Church of England graveyard.

Charles Wesley was a man of integrity and sincerity, although impulsive and hot-headed at times. He was a passionate and dynamic preacher who played his part in the spiritual revival of the eighteenth century. George Whitefield thought him to be the best preacher in England, even better than John. But like his brother, Charles was courageous in the face of violence and genuine in his love for the lost without Christ.

A well-educated and intelligent man, Charles was most importantly a man who loved the Scriptures and knew them well. Above all he was a gifted poet and a highly acclaimed hymn writer.

The Methodist Conference of 1788 paid tribute to Charles with these words: 'Mr Charles Wesley, who after spending four score years with much sorrow and pain, quietly retired into Abraham's bosom. He had no disease, but after gradual decay of some months "the weary wheels of life stood still at last."'

John's Itinerary did not ease up. He continued to work hard for the Lord, although he could no longer accept all the invitations he received to preach.

Every morning, he rose at four o'clock and went through the main duties of the day with his companion, an Irishman called Henry Moore, who lived with him at this time. John's constant prayer was, 'Lord, let me not live to be useless.'

There was of course one last visit to Ireland in 1789 and then on New Year's Day in 1790, John wrote an honest journal entry.

> 'I am now an old man, decayed from hand to foot. My eyes are dim; my right hand shakes much; my mouth is hot and dry every morning; I have a lingering fever almost every day; my motion is weak and slow. However, blessed be God, I do not slack my labour: I can preach and write still.'[3]

The rest of that year was taken up with speaking engagements across the length and breadth of England. At every place he visited, he gave the Methodist Society in that area one final piece of advice: 'To love as brethren, fear God and honour the king.'

John preached in the open air for the last time on 6 October, 1790, under a large ash tree near a ruined church building at Winchelsea in east Sussex.

---

3. John Wesley's *Journal*, Volume 4, page 478, entry for Friday 1 January, 1790.

'The kingdom of God is at hand; repent and believe in the gospel,'[4] John proclaimed to a large congregation in a clear and commanding voice. 'Repentance is a change of mind that leads to a change of loyalty. And that, Christ Jesus says, is what we must do. We must change our minds from ignoring him and going our own way. We must acknowledge that he is the Christ, the Son of God. As we trust him, as we surrender our lives willingly to Jesus the King of kings, so we discover that his message is truly good news.'

It was a powerful sermon that day. John noticed that all who listened carefully were 'almost persuaded to be Christians.'[5]

Two and a half weeks later John made his final entry into his journal. On 22 February, 1791, he preached his last sermon in a house in Leatherhead, about seventeen miles south of the centre of London. Two days after that, he wrote his final letter. It was to the great anti-slave trade campaigner, William Wilberforce.[6]

When they were in America, John and Charles had become familiar with the horrors of slavery. By 1774, John strongly protested against the slave trade and all who took part in it. He wrote his 'Thoughts Upon Slavery' and published it. The following year he published *Calm Address to our American Colonies* on the evils of slavery.

---

4. Mark 1:15.

5. John Wesley's *Journal*, Volume 4, page 496, entry for Tuesday, 7 October, 1790.

6. See the *Fact File* called, 'John Wesley's Letter to William Wilberforce', at the back of the book.

John threatened slave traders with a worse outcome than Sodom and Gomorrah.[7] He reminded them that, 'Judgement is without mercy to one who has shown no mercy.'[8] He told plantation owners that, '*Men-buyers* are exactly on a level with *men-stealers.*' He told merchants that their money was being used, 'To steal, rob, murder men, women, and children without number.'

Yes, it seemed good to John that he should write to encourage the young Mr Wilberforce in his mission to abolish the wicked practice altogether.

Shortly after eleven o'clock on the morning of Friday, 25 February, 1791, John went to lie down for a while at his residence in City Road, London. His pulse was rapid, and he had a fever. Some friends gathered around him, to keep him company and to pray for him.

Over the weekend, his strength waned. All John could do from his bed was repeat the words of a hymn written by Isaac Watts[9], 'I'll praise my maker while I've breath.' Occasionally he would exclaim, 'The best of all is, God is with us!'

On the morning of John's death, his niece, Sarah Wesley, and a few friends knelt by his bedside. Sarah gently took her uncle's hand. Then she looked at the grave faces of her praying friends. They all knew that his time was short.

---

7. Genesis 19:24-25.

8. James 2:13.

9. *Isaac Watts* was born on 17 July, 1674 and died on 25 November, 1748. After his education, he was a minister in an English Congregational church in London and a hymn writer.

Just before ten o'clock in the morning of Wednesday, 2 March 1791, John quietly muttered, 'Farewell' to the praying friends at his bedside. Then he died.

The funeral service was held in City Road Chapel a week later. John had left written instructions in his will that,

> 'There may be no hearse, no coach, no shield bearing a coat of arms, no pomp, except the tears of them that loved me and are following me to Abraham's bosom.'[10]

His instructions were faithfully followed.

During the words of committal, the sobbing from the mourners got louder and louder. John's body was laid in a vault which he had prepared for himself.

John Wesley was a man of great faith and ability. Not only was he full of passion, commitment, and energy, he was also a magnificent organiser. The Methodist Societies that he and Charles established, gave their members a degree of social security and purpose – to grow in Christlikeness and proclaim his gospel to the lost.

Methodism helped to influence the moral principles of a nation and benefitted society generally. Their Sunday Schools improved education amongst children.

The influence of John and Charles was to extend beyond their own lifetimes. Today there are tens of millions of Methodists all over the world.

---

10. John Wesley's *Journal*, Volume 4, page 501, entry from his last 'Will and Testament'.

The writing on John's tomb captures accurately not only his life, but the life of his brother Charles as well:

This GREAT LIGHT arose
(By the singular Providence of God)
To enlighten THESE NATIONS,
And to *revive, enforce and defend,*
The Pure Apostolic DOCTRINES and PRACTICES of
THE PRIMITIVE CHURCH:
Which he continued to do, both by his WRITINGS
and his LABOURS
For more than HALF A CENTURY:
And to his inexpressible Joy,
Not only, beheld their INFLUENCE extending,
And their EFFICACY witness'd,
In the Hearts and Lives of MANY THOUSANDS,
As well in THE WESTERN WORLD as in
THESE KINGDOMS:
But also far above all human Power of Expectation,
Liv'd to see PROVISION made by the singular
Grace of GOD,
For their CONTINUANCE and ESTABLISHMENT,
TO THE JOY OF FUTURE GENERATIONS,
READER If thou art constrained to bless
the INSTRUMENT,
GIVE GOD THE GLORY.

Fact Files

The Moravians

The Moravians evolved from the Hussite movement led by John Hus (1369-1415). Hus rejected some teachings and practices of the Roman Catholic Church. In 1722, a handful of refugees fled from the province of Moravia, now in the Czech Republic, to escape persecution. They were given shelter in Switzerland by a Lutheran nobleman called Count von Zinzendorf.

The Moravians were a peaceful people who condemned all violence including capital punishment, service in war, or even swearing oaths to earthly authorities. They placed a great deal of importance on unity, personal devotion, mission, and music.

Hymns and Poems

In 1737 John Wesley published his first hymn book: *A Collection of Psalms and Hymns*. It contained seventy hymns written by various authors and five were translated from German by John himself.

John and Charles later published several hymn books in their joint names, called *Hymns and Sacred Poems* in 1739, 1742 (three separate books); and then a two volume work in 1749.

Charles wrote the majority of the hymns and John edited them into what we sing today. In fact, Charles Wesley wrote more than 9,000 hymns and poems in his lifetime. In 1762, Charles published his magnum opus, *Short Hymns on Selected Passages of Scripture* – 2 Volumes containing 2,030 hymns.

The following song by Charles was probably inspired by Galatians 2:20 – 'The life I now live in the flesh I live by faith in the Son of God, who loved me and gave himself for me.' The last two lines of each stanza are sung twice.

> And can it be that I should gain
> An int'rest in the Saviour's blood?
> Died he for me, who caused his pain;
> For me, who him to death pursued?
> Amazing love! how can it be
> That thou, my God, shouldst die for me?
>
> He left his Father's throne above—
> So free, so infinite his grace—
> Emptied himself of all but love,
> And bled for Adam's helpless race.
> 'Tis mercy all, immense and free;
> For, O my God, it found out me!
>
> Long my imprisoned spirit lay
> Fast bound in sin and nature's night:
> Thine eye diffused a quickening ray—
> I woke, the dungeon flamed with light;
> My chains fell off, my heart was free.
> I rose, went forth, and followed thee.
>
> No condemnation now I dread;
> Jesus, and all in him is mine!
> Alive in him, my living head,
> And clothed in righteousness divine,
> Bold I approach the eternal throne,
> And claim the crown, through Christ, my own.
>
> Charles Wesley (1707-88)

It is believed that Charles composed this song in the farmhouse at Killyleagh, Northern Ireland:

> Jesu, lover of my soul,
> Let me to thy bosom fly,
> While the nearest waters roll,
> While the tempest still is high;
> Hide me, O my Saviour, hide,
> Till the storm of life be past;
> Safe into the haven guide,
> O receive my soul at last.
> Other refuge have I none,
> Hangs my helpless soul on thee;
> Leave, ah leave me not alone,
> Still support and comfort me;
> All my trust on thee is stayed,
> All my help from thee I bring;
> Cover my defenceless head
> With the shadow of thy wing.
>
> Thou, O Christ, art all I want;
> More than all in thee I find;
> Raise the fallen, cheer the faint,
> Heal the sick, and lead the blind;
> Just and holy is thy name,
> I am all unrighteousness;
> False and full of sin I am,
> Thou art full of truth and grace.
>
> Plenteous grace with thee is found,
> Grace to cover all my sin;
> Let the healing streams abound:
> Make and keep me pure within.
> Thou of life the fountain art,
> Freely let me take of thee,
> Spring thou up within my heart,
> Rise to all eternity.

Charles Wesley (1707-88)

Charles also wrote some wonderful Christmas carols. Probably the most famous one is this:

HARK! the herald angels sing
Glory to the newborn King;
Peace on earth and mercy mild,
God and sinners reconciled!
Joyful, all you nations rise,
Join the triumph of the skies;
With the angelic host proclaim,
'Christ is born in Bethlehem':

HARK! The herald angels sing
Glory to the new-born King.

Christ, by highest heaven adored,
Christ, the everlasting Lord;
Late in time behold him come,
Offspring of a virgin's womb:
Veiled in flesh the Godhead see,
Hail the incarnate Deity!
Pleased as man with us to dwell,
Jesus our Emmanuel:

HARK! The herald angels sing
Glory to the new-born King.

Hail, the heaven-born Prince of Peace!
Hail, the Sun of righteousness!
Light and life to all he brings,
Risen with healing in his wings:
Mild, he lays his glory by,
Born that we no more may die;
Born to raise each child of earth
Born to give us second birth:

HARK! The herald angels sing
Glory to the new-born King.

Charles Wesley (1707-88)

The Conventicle Acts in
Seventeenth Century England

The Conventicle Acts of 1662, 1664 and 1670 did not allow for the reading of prayers at 'conventicles' – this was the term given to gatherings of people who wanted to worship God in places other than in Church of England churches. It was a crime to be involved in a 'conventicle'. Anyone caught being part of a 'conventicle' could be fined and thrown into prison.

The purpose of the Conventicle Acts was to force people to attend services in Church of England churches. The Toleration Act of 1689 allowed Protestants who were not members of the Church of England to worship together, but they had to register with the government as 'Dissenters'. They had to make certain oaths of allegiance. 'Disenters' were also excluded from holding any political office or attending universities.

Controversies

'The Calvinistic Controversy'

The initial outbreak of the 'Calvinistic Controversy' in 1740 led to the separation of George Whitefield and the Wesleys. The division also formed two distinct parties within the Methodist movement.

The problem was called 'The Calvinistic Controversy' because there was disagreement concerning the Biblical doctrine of election (also known as *predestination*). The controversary took its name from a French theologian called John Calvin

(1509-1564), who was the greatest advocate of the doctrine of election during the sixteenth century Reformation in Europe.

Calvin believed the Bible taught clearly that before the creation of the world, God chose many people to be saved in Christ. They are saved not because they are especially good or amazing, but because of God's sovereign good pleasure. Others he has left to their own hardened hearts and rebellion.

God has mercy on some, drawing them to Christ – that is grace. And God hardens the hearts of those who are happy to harden their own hearts against him. They have willingly become the slaves of the devil, and that is judgement.[1]

George Whitefield and his followers in the Methodist movement were called 'Calvinists' because they agreed with John Calvin's teaching about election.

John and Charles Wesley were 'Arminians' in belief because they followed the teaching of Jacobus Arminius (1560-1609), who was a Dutch theologian. Arminius believed that salvation was available to all but not accepted by all because God had given humanity the free will to choose salvation for themselves.

The Wesleys were not aware that John Calvin did preach about the love of God for all people. 'Jesus Christ offers himself generally to all [people] without

---

1. For example, in Romans 1, the people were futile in their thinking, their hearts were hard, and in God's judgment, they were *given over* by God to indulge their sin.

exception to be their redeemer' and that 'love ... extends to all [people], inasmuch as Jesus Christ reaches out his arms to call and allure all [people] both great and small, to win them to him' (Calvin, *Sermons on Deuteronomy*; Calvin's Commentary on John 3:16).

When George Whitefield wrote to John Wesley that 'God is loving to every man', John Wesley admitted that he never understood Whitefield's 'Calvinism'.

Nonetheless, the Wesleys adamantly resisted the 'Calvinist' view of *election* all their lives.

'Christian Perfection'

In one of his sermons, John proclaimed that, 'Christians are saved in this world from all sin, from all unrighteousness, that they are now in such a sense perfect, and to be freed from evil thoughts and evil tempers.'[2]

In other words, once a person is made right with God, they do not sin anymore.

The danger of 'Christian Perfection' is that it can produce moral permissiveness and self-indulgence in the life of the church.

Of course John and Charles were not teaching people to be ungodly. They often emphasised the need for holiness in the Christian's life. However, throughout their ministries, they wrote about

---

2. From John Wesley's sermon called 'Christian Perfection', in *John Wesley's Forty-Four Sermons*, Epworth Press, point II, paragraph 28, page 476.

'Christian perfection' in tracts, and preached about it in their sermons.[3]

Bishop J.C. Ryle (1816-1900) spoke affectionately about John Wesley, but his words could equally be attributed to Charles Wesley:

> 'The founder of Methodism was a man of no mean reputation in Oxford, and his writings show him to have been a well-read, logical minded, and intelligent man. He was a bold fighter on Christ's side, a fearless warrior against sin, the world and the devil, and an unflinching adherent of the Lord Jesus Christ in a very dark day. He honoured the Bible. He cried down sin. He made much of Christ's blood. He exalted holiness. He taught the absolute need of repentance, faith, and conversion. Surely these things ought not to be forgotten. Let us thank God for a mighty instrument in God's hand for good.'[4]

---

3. For example, 'Sermon XXXV on Christian Perfection', John Wesley's *Forty Four Sermons,* Epworth, pages 457-480.

4. J.C. Ryle, *Christian Leaders of the 18ᵗʰ Century*, Banner of Truth, pages 104-105.

John and Charles Wesley Timeline

1703	John Wesley born.
1707	Charles Wesley born.
1714	John went to Charterhouse School.
1716	Charles went to Westminster School.
1720	John entered Christ Church, Oxford.
1725	John started to keep a detailed diary.
	John was ordained deacon by Dr John Potter, Bishop of Oxford.
1726	John elected Fellow of Lincoln College, Oxford.
	Charles enrolled at Christ Church, Oxford.
	Sarah (Sally) Gwynne was born.
1727	John became Curate of Epworth and Wroot.
1728	John was ordained priest by Dr John Potter, Bishop of Oxford.
1729	Charles began to keep a diary.
	Holy Club formed. John returned to Oxford and took over leadership of the Holy Club.
1730	Charles became a tutor at Oxford.
1732	The Holy Club becomes known as Methodists.
	George Whitefield introduced to the Holy Club.
	The colony of Georgia established in America.
1735	Samuel Wesley, rector of Epworth, died.
	Charles was ordained deacon.
	Charles was appointed Secretary for Indian Affairs in Georgia.
	Charles was ordained priest.
1736	John and Charles began ministry in Georgia.
	Charles left Georgia.
1737	John fled Savannah for England.

1738	John landed in Deal, England.
	Charles experienced 'conversion' to Christ.
	John experienced 'conversion' to Christ.
1739	John started open-air field preaching.
	Charles first preached in fields.
	Their brother, Samuel Wesley, died.
1742	Their mother, Mrs Susanna Wesley, died.
	Methodism spread rapidly through England.
1747	John and Charles began their work in Ireland.
1749	Charles married Sally Gwynne.
1751	John married Molly Vazeille.
	John visited Scotland for the first time and preached at Musselburgh.
1757	Charles' son, also called Charles, was born.
1759	Charles' daughter Sarah was born.
1762	Charles published: *Short Hymns on Selected Passages of Scripture* – 2 Volumes with 2,030 hymns.
1766	Charles' son Samuel was born.
1770	George Whitefield died in Massachusetts, America.
1771	Charles, Sally and family moved to Chesterfield Street in Marylebone, London.
1774	John published his *Thoughts Upon Slavery*.
1775	John published *Calm Address to our American Colonies* on the evils of slavery.
1781	Molly Wesley died in London.
1784	John ordained Dr Thomas Coke to oversee the Methodist work in America.
1788	Charles Wesley died in Marylebone, London.
1791	John Wesley died in City Road, London.
1822	Sally Wesley died in Marylebone, London.

Thinking Further Topics

Chapter One – Fire! Fire!

When the Wesley home went on fire Mr Wesley prayed. How do you react in a crisis? Read Acts 12:5 to see how the church in Jerusalem reacted to a crisis it was facing.

Chapter Two – A Good Education

Every morning John read the Bible but paid little attention to it. Was he being a good Christian by doing this? Read James 1:22-25.

Chapter Three – The Holy Club

The Wesleys talked to prisoners about Jesus. Was that right? Surely criminals have rejected Jesus. Should we talk to them about Jesus? Read Romans 3:10-18, 23.

Chapter Four – Storms at Sea

The storms at sea caused a crisis of faith for John and Charles. When challenges crash over you do you trust in Jesus? Read 2 Corinthians 4:14-18 and Romans 8:18.

Chapter Five – Secretary For Indian Affairs

Charles' first ministry failed; partly because he was not converted. What did Charles preach about how to get to heaven? Do you believe you can get to heaven through things that you do? (Galatians 2:16)

Chapter Six – Chaplain In Savannah

John wanted to tell the natives about God, but they were too busy fighting. Are you too busy for God? Read Acts 2:42 and Hebrews 10:24-25.

Chapter Seven – My Chains Fell Off

John and Charles realised that it is by God's grace alone that anyone can be saved. Are you saved? Read John 3:16, Ephesians 2:8-9, and Acts 4:12.

Chapter Eight – Preaching Outdoors

When John preached in the open air he taught from

Luke 4:18-19 where Jesus read from the prophet Isaiah. What did Jesus say he had come to do? How did the people respond? How do you respond to Jesus? Read Isaiah 61:1-2 and Luke 4:16-30.

Chapter Nine – In The Mission Field

John reminded himself in his journal to keep proclaiming the gospel even when there was no sign of fruit. Do you still tell people about Jesus, or have you given up? Read Mark 4:1-20 and 1 Corinthians 3:6-7.

Chapter Ten – Riots and Opposition

Even under the threat of violence John would tell people about God's love. How do you react when angry people threaten you because you tell them about Jesus? Read John 15:18, 1 John 3:13 and Colossians 3:23-25.

Chapter Eleven – Across the Irish Sea

Under threat from a crowd, Charles began to compose a hymn of praise to Jesus. Do you praise the Lord even in difficulty? Read Psalms 42–43 and Psalm 95.

Chapter Twelve – Love and Marriage

Charles and John got married. Read Genesis 2:24, Proverbs 31:10-12, Matthew 19:4-6, 1 Corinthians 7:2-9, 2 Corinthians 6:14-17 and Ephesians 5:21-31 to find out about a good Christian marriage.

Chapter Thirteen – A Time Of Grief

The Wesley brothers mourned the death of George Whitefield. They sometimes disagreed but were still brothers-in-Christ. How was that possible? Consider Psalm 133:1, Ephesians 4:1-3, and 1 Peter 3:8-9.

Chapter Fourteen – Give God The Glory

Charles and John died in old age but did not grow weary in serving Jesus. Do you get tired from serving God in your life? How might you keep going till the end? Read 2 Corinthians 4:14-5:10, and Hebrews 12:1-3.